# CLASSIC GARDEN FEATURES

# CLASSIC
# GARDEN
# FEATURES

David Stuart

conran
OCTOPUS

**HALF TITLE** *A lichen-encrusted lion, probably late eighteenth century, dozes in a garden. Such animals, usually one of a pair, have been commonly found flanking doorways and flights of steps since the Renaissance. Nineteenth-century gardeners loved them too, and vast numbers were cast in iron, terracotta, and even in concrete. Modern ones are variable in quality, but the best can be exceptional.*

**TITLE PAGE** *One of the great North American garden classics, Adirondack seats were first made in the second half of the nineteenth century for the country houses of New York's wealthy. Here, a seat looks out on the view from a garden in the Hamptons. They are now made by companies all over the United States, and though simply constructed, they are extremely comfortable.*

**LEFT** *Shells used as garden decoration were popular in seventeenth- and eighteenth-century grottos, often as part of a fountain. Here is a modern update from Spain: shells, nailed to a wall, are used as containers and sport Crassula arborescens and Aloe africana. Epiphytic orchids and bromeliads would be good too.*

**RIGHT** *Handsome satyrs like this have been spouting since Roman times. This fine example in cast lead, popular in the nineteenth century, looks splendid against the leaden scales of his wall.*

# CONTENTS

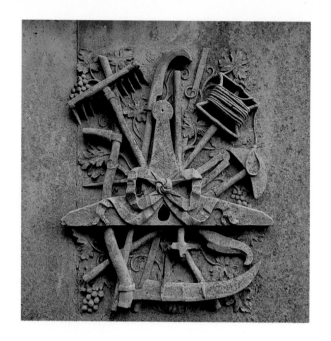

**RIGHT** *This horticultural trophy is at Hall Barn, Buckinghamshire, a garden well-known since the early eighteenth century. A swagger piece of eighteenth-century stone carving, it shows garden implements including a scythe, edging spade, garden line (used for planting bulbs or seedlings in straight rows) and a billhook, fancifully tied together with ribbons and vines.*

**CENTRE** *A herculean figure at Chatsworth, Derbyshire, makes a dramatic centrepiece to this theatrical view, framed by formal beech hedges. It is possible to create as much drama in tiny gardens by applying the same principle, but using a more modest central feature, perhaps a reproduction urn, a large container, or a piece of contemporary statuary.*

**FAR RIGHT** *Topiary standards, closely clipped box hedges, and natural gravels, make this subtle pattern at Moseley Old Hall, Staffordshire. Here, the natural shades of gravel for the separate areas are perfectly matched; some seventeenth-century gardeners tried more colourful materials such as crushed brick, yellow sand, coal dust, and even the coloured tesserae used for mosaics.*

# AN INTRODUCTION TO CLASSIC GARDEN STYLE

Since their beginning, gardens have been structured and defined by enclosing walls and access paths. Originating with the first settled cultures in parched Mesopotamia, they have also needed water reservoirs as well as water sources and their gardeners have created places to shelter from the sun, and to sit and rest. Gardeners have experimented with new and exciting plants, and have needed containers like pots, baskets, and tubs, in which to transport them to new locations, or in which to grow them. Walls, paths, containers, water tanks, pergolas, and seats became garden features as soon as they played a role in the garden's design. Yet, amid the tumble of plants, gardeners have also wanted some visual focus to the garden too, whether an image of the garden's god, a life-bringing fountain, or even something as simple as a sundial.

All these garden features have been used to express a garden's style and quite often the garden owner's status. Many are purely functional, while others, such as sculpture and topiary, provide decorative interest. A classic garden feature is one that encapsulates a garden style, or an epoch of gardening, in the way that a formal trellis panel can sum up a Parisian courtyard garden; an Adirondack chair can transport the gardener to a shady nineteenth-century North American terrace; or a Japanese stone

lantern to a bamboo and paeony edged path, winding towards a sixteenth-century tea house. Great classic features of this quality have been created by almost all garden cultures, from the scalloped marble fountains of Moorish Spain to the moon gates of sixteenth-century China. Victorian Britain produced the cast-iron and classic *tazza*-shaped urns now found all over Europe and North America, while nineteenth-century France first produced classic filigree wirework plant stands and hanging baskets.

Classic features, too, are inevitably garden elements with a long, sometimes an immensely long, history. They have been used in gardens that range from the formal to cottage and kitchen gardens, and they have given many different gardeners great delight. Features range from the grand to the modest, and from the most ancient to those at the leading edge of contemporary design and technology. All the basic concepts, whether plant support, lamp, seat, statue, fountain or container, however modern, would have been immediately recognized by gardeners throughout history, and from every continent.

Classic features also generally travel well. In the 1880s, and for the next few decades, Japanese dipping wells and stone lanterns were sent from Japan to hundreds

of gardens in Europe and North America, and many look almost as well set among unfamiliar firs and rhododendrons as they once did in their native land. The English architect Edwin Lutyens designed his classic early twentieth-century wooden garden seat to be set in the luscious herbaceous borders of the English home counties, but the Lutyens seat, based on some seventeenth-century chinoiserie originals, looks quite as good in gardens in Maine or Queensland.

Perhaps the reason for this is that the art of gardening began at the very start of civilization, and is completely entwined with human history. Almost all the features in the garden, and many of its plants, are as old as gardening, and as much part of ourselves. That can, perhaps, be a disadvantage, for it puts the burden of an immense and sumptuously rich history on any gardener, designer or craftsman, who tries to do something completely new.

It is not surprising that modern classics are inevitably reinterpretations of much older ideas. These reinterpretations are often based on a new technology, or on a new material. Modern lighting techniques, used imaginatively, can give a garden every bit as much magic as the light from a flaring torch; modern electric motors, quiet and

**LEFT** *Though modern low-voltage lighting can create magical effects in the garden, candlelight is perfect too. To keep the breeze from the flame, glass storm lanterns, Spanish or Moroccan tin lanterns, Chinese lanterns, or contemporary wire-mesh lanterns like these, give an entirely classical mood to the garden.*

**CENTRE** *At Denmans, in West Sussex, in a garden designed by writer and designer John Brookes, seating is reduced to its simplest form – a log propped on supports at each end. It is a good place to rest beneath the old fruit trees, but though romantic to look at, gardeners through the ages have invented more comfortable seats.*

**FAR LEFT** *An unusual topping for a garden pole, this campana-shaped urn is painted white, a popular colour for these urns in the late nineteenth century. The pole would make a good support for pale pink climbing roses, perhaps sumptuous 'Blairii Number Two'.*

unobtrusive, allow gardens to have fountains and rills that would have been impossible a few decades ago, but whose designs almost always echo ancient ideas.

Ancient, modern, or even just plain old-fashioned, classic features are all strong visual statements in the garden. They are mostly static and season-less, man-made and beautiful. They make an exciting juxtaposition with the burgeoning natural life of the plants, and by contrasting with that organic magic, create their own excitement. Nevertheless, for all the emphasis on features, and on their fascinating history, plants are still the key to the garden.

Cram pools with waterlilies, lotuses, or wonderful Japanese irises. Fill the working garden with vegetables and fruit trees, and cover the potting shed with runner beans or some of the numerous varieties of French ones. Fill containers with glorious tulips, or cascades of verbenas. If your garden will not support lemon trees, fill Versailles tubs with double white daturas, or even tougher oleanders. Grow blue morning glory up indigo obelisks, and surround them with drifts of rust-brown irises, with violet asters for autumn. Smother walls and pergolas with vines. And only then choose a classic seat from these pages, and sit down to admire your creation.

# WATER FEATURES

# WATER, THE SOUL OF EVERY GARDEN

In the gardens of 6,000 years ago, water was life itself. Water was sacred, and inhabited by the gods. Water was power, and who controlled its supply was powerful. Early gardens in Mesopotamia were based on a map of the known world. Each garden was divided into quarters, with four water channels meeting at a central tank.

Three thousand years later, in ancient Iran, colossal resources were spent to supply cities, farms and gardens with water. The system of *quanats* was in place by 600 BC. These astonishing tunnels channelled water from mountains to cities on the plain. Some are still in working order. Later, the Romans built immense aqueducts to supply water to their cities, where grand public fountains proclaimed the wealth of the state.

Even in lands where water was more abundant, it was still sacred and a source of power. The ancient Chinese regarded it as the soul of the garden and built artificial lakes from 300 BC. In South America, the Mayans built ceremonial pools, while the Mogul princes of India filled their gardens with fountains. In their time, Renaissance Italians, seventeenth-century French aristocrats and European kings competed to produce the most glorious water features and the most sumptuous mirror-like sheets of water.

Gardeners all over the world are still fascinated by water. New technology means that we can have fountains and waterfalls even if we own only a few square metres of garden. Great cities and industrial corporations still build cascades and fountains for the enjoyment of their public. The Fort Worth Water Garden and the Bank of China gardens in Hong Kong are stupendous examples of modern classicism. But every private gardener can have, however tiny the garden, a water feature.

**OVERLEAF** *This high arched form of bridge originated in ancient China. Such bridges were designed for visual effect as well as transportation. The* Mustard Seed Manual, *(1679) a Chinese garden design manual, suggests crossing bridges as an event to be savoured, suspending the traveller between earth, water and air. This one spans water in North America.*

**RIGHT** *A simple classic lead spigot spouting water into a marble basin is one of the oldest of all garden features. Here, a modern spigot pours into an antique marble tank, which overflows to feed a lower tank. Fenton House, in Hampstead Grove, London, was built in the seventeenth century, and parts of the garden are of the same date. A feature like this suits small, formal layouts well, especially on one side of a small courtyard, or at a path end.*

RIGHT *This handsome classical mask is at Coton Manor, Ravensthorpe, in Northamptonshire. He is full of classic energy, with stylized hair and beard, and dates from the mid-nineteenth century. In Roman times, spigot masks were often of Bacchus, and water springs have long been associated with minor deities.*

# THE POWER OF MOVING WATER

Moving water expresses power in a very tangible way. Not only can it devastate, at a stroke, the puny works of humans, but can also, when tamed, work mills and turbines, and power whole cities. In the garden, water has, for centuries, been used to express wealth and power, as it does at Versailles in France, Peterhof in Russia and many other great palaces of Europe.

Water features in gardens are an ancient tradition. By the sixth century BC, Cyrus the Great, King of Persia, built palaces and gardens at Pasargadae, now in Iran. The inside of these sumptuous palaces were cooled by formal watercourses which continued to flow uninterrupted out into the gardens. These colossal watercourses were constructed of large oblong tanks carved from single blocks of limestone. The tanks were linked by narrow runnels and were over a 1,000m (3,280ft) in length. Such was their success that the idea of great water tanks linked by straight rills went on to influence gardens for

**LEFT** *The enchanting baroque garden at Rosendael Park, now in the care of the State, near Arnhem, in the Netherlands was built by Jan van Arnhem in the 1660s. Though much of it was turned into a landscape park in the eighteenth century, the shell grottos and the linear avenues were kept. Here, a miniature ceramic water stair, almost a* chadar, *sits among flowers made of shells.*

another two millennia. The water garden at Buscot Park in Oxfordshire is an excellent example of one created in the twentieth century.

In ancient Rhodes, the Greeks had courtyards with fountains, and almost all gardens of the Roman Empire were filled with water features, from basic spouts (sometimes issuing from a satyr's bearded face), to water staircases, and fountain-girt pools. Some of the grandest domestic water features of ancient Rome have been found in the Portuguese city of Conimbriga. There, every courtyard had an elaborately shaped pool, often surrounded by many tiny fountains, covered in gorgeous mosaics. Each courtyard also had planting beds, which, archaeology shows, were for figs, vines and lemons. Wall paintings show vines, myrtles, curious clipped domes of ivy, many wild animals, fountains and ponds. They would make a lovely planting today.

Water staircases, which give water sound and keep the air cool and moist, were popular in Middle Eastern gardens at the beginning of the last millennium, where they became extremely elaborate. Called *chadars*, their slopes are often of intricately carved marble, sometimes with tiny covered niches for lamps. Some are big, though none more glamorous than the one in tenth-century Moorish Toledo, Spain. In that city, *chadars* formed the roof of a pavilion of gold and glass. The water poured down the dome to make curtains of tumbling water.

In Europe, water staircases became an integral part of the grotto, where they could be made shallow but steep, and take up little floor space. However, gardeners soon realized that they made perfect wall features in the open garden too, and they can be found emerging from screens of ivy, moss and ferns, all over Europe. In today's gardens they are built of all sorts of materials, from old water cisterns, to galvanized buckets. Easy to build, they can be great fun, and do not take up much space in the garden.

In 1404, the great khan Tamerlane, received ambassadors from Europe in his palace in Samarkand, in Uzbekistan. They were astonished to see him seated on a shaded dais by a marble tank with fountains. Tamerlane's descendants built themselves magnificent water-filled gardens where canals fed cascades and fountains, and tiled or marble pavilions sat in the middle of vast tanks of clear water. They cared for flowers too, and the emperor Babur himself planted *Bauhinia variegata* around his favourite fountains, and surrounded others with parterres of scarlet and purple anemones, or pomegranates and pineapples, and hollyhocks and tuberoses.

All early fountains were fed by closed water channels built beside or beneath the main water feature. These were unable to withstand high water pressures, so the height of the water spout in gardens was limited, including those in Saracen gardens, whose

influence the Crusaders brought to Europe in the twelfth century. Though medieval European gardeners wanted fountains too, similar constraints applied until lead technology developed sufficiently in the late sixteenth century when piping became available with sufficient strength to enable much bigger jets of water to adorn gardens.

Competitive water engineering developed rapidly in sixteenth-century Italy, and the science of hydraulics developed fast. There were even professional fountaineers.

FAR RIGHT *Among the most beautiful of all gardens near Rome is Villa Lante, at Viterbo. This water stair is part of the scheme started in the 1580s. As the water tumbles downhill cooling the air, its sound mixes with that of the dozens of fountains in this enchanting garden. Here, the water pours from the claws of a giant crayfish, the emblem of owner Cardinal Gambara. At Villa Caprarola, also near Rome, a rival cardinal built a version of the fountain flanked by dolphins.*

RIGHT *Peter the Great's ultimate water feature, Peterhof, near St Petersburg, is an assemblage of 75 fountains. It stands at the end of a 600m (1,968ft) canal that stretches from the Gulf of Finland to his summer palace. Though he designed the canal himself, the cascades and fountains are by architects le Blond and Marchetti. The centrepiece is the great Samson Fountain, where Samson pulls apart the jaws of a lion representing Sweden, whose army Peter had just defeated. Of gilded bronze, lead and marble, the water first glittered here in 1723.*

Tommaso Francini started work in France in the 1590s, and his offspring became hereditary fountaineers to the kings of France. They retained their unique and privileged position until the French Revolution. The palaces of Versailles, the Trianon and Marly had between them 1,400 fountains. Versailles had the most. In the great *fête* of 1688, its fountains disgorged more water than the whole population of Paris could use in the same time, and the city had 60,000 inhabitants. Other European rulers felt the need to compete with the French kings, and many vast and grandiose water gardens were created in the eighteenth century, especially in Italy and Russia.

In terms of sheer height though, it was an English aristocrat who won the glory. Using the latest cast-iron technology, the Duke of Devonshire employed his gardener Joseph Paxton to build the Emperor Fountain at Chatsworth. The fountain was put in place by 1842, and, serviced by a distant tank and a huge amount of strong piping, it still spouts to an amazing 80.6m (267ft), without the help of an electric motor. Nowadays, fountains of all sizes are driven by electric motors, and the smallest garden can have a stone satyr that spouts water, or several tiny fountains that echo the gardens of ancient Rome, or distant Samarkand.

**RIGHT**  *This handsome Australian water garden shows how something entirely modern can use some of the language of the past, and have all the serenity of classic Japanese or Islamic gardens. The delicate planting of papyrus and marsilea are a perfect foil to the high water level and the crispness of the design.*

# THE SERENITY OF STILL WATER

As well as showing pomp, glory and movement, water can also be still, contemplative and mysterious. It can cast reflections like a mirror, and gardeners have always used waterside features to demonstrate the perfection of the mirror and the beauty of the view. These features include sculptures, lanterns, pavilions and bridges.

As with moving water, all garden cultures have admired water at rest. All ancient Chinese gardens have still water: the lake at the Palace of Glorious Purity, near Sian, still reflects crimson and green pavilions in its greeny waters. In China, water is rich with symbolism, and thought to represent the highest virtue. That, said Lao Tzu, the founder of Taoism, is because it yields but can engulf, is modest but wears away stones. Chinese landscapers considered water the blood of heaven and earth, and water was central to

ABOVE *Though the garden at
Tatton Park, Knutsford, in
Cheshire, has many marvellous
features, the best was built
following the third Lord Egerton's
visit to the Japanese Exhibition of
1905. He fell in love with the
idea of a Japanese garden and the
one he created remains the best in
the country. The scheme is centred
on a thatched teahouse. A
charming zigzag bridge of
flagstones emerges from dense
plantings of Japanese irises.*

every garden, even the small ones of Chinese civil servants (though they were artists, poets, scholars and calligraphers as well as administrators).

Bridges were important garden features in both China and Japan, sometimes mimicking the great engineering triumphs such as the high-arching timber Kintai Bridge at Iwakuni, Japan, or the lovely covered pavilion bridge at the ancient Kyoto garden of Shugaku-in. Some had pergolas along their length to give wisterias a perfect place to display themselves. Nearer to the surface of the water, wooden or stone zigzag bridges were created to make the delightful moment of traversing water last longer; zigzag stepping stones gave the crossing a touch of excitement too. Either of these methods of crossing water can look perfect in modern gardens, especially if they emerge from beautiful plantings of Japanese irises and ligularias.

Eastern gardens have provided today's gardens around the world with many other classic water and waterside features. The Japanese tea ceremony, a ritual that started in the sixteenth century, has been especially important in the development of

garden design. Stone, or more rarely bronze, lanterns lit the way along mossy paths to the tea house, often placed so that they would be reflected in the water. There were many forms; perhaps the most beautiful are those with broad roof stones, designed to catch snow and hold fringes of icicles. Lanterns were also placed to light the water basin, or laver, with its bamboo dipper. These were near the tea house, often at the end of a side path, and the water arrived through bamboo pipes. The stone troughs were commonly set in a bed of gravel to allow the overflowing water to drain away. A traditional planting around such a trough always included some Japanese maples (*Acer japonicum*); heavenly bamboo (*Nandina domestica*) (also with wonderful autumn colour); clipped Sasa bamboos; Japanese apricot (*Prunus mume*), a lovely apricot that flowers as soon as winter is over, and the Chinese persimmon (*Diospyros kaki*).

Still water could be found in the Middle East too, though the prime emphasis was always on water in movement. In the ninth century, ambassadors from Byzantium were sent to the Caliph at Baghdad. They were amazed at the Caliph's garden where 400 palm trees, their trunks encased in carved teak and gilded brass, surrounded a vast rectangular pool. Formal planting immediately surrounding a formal piece of water is still marvellously effective.

In the West, the liking for still water in the garden was less marked. There are still pools at the Emperor Hadrian's villa at Tivoli, quite close to Rome in Italy, but the great age of magnificent still stretches of water in Europe really started in France in the sixteenth century. The first great canal was dug at Fleury. Its beauty inspired the French king Henri IV to excavate the Grand Canal at Fontainebleau nearby. That marvellous piece of water was begun in 1607, towards the end of Henri's reign and, surrounded by its dark forests, still looks good today.

*LEFT Bronze cranes like these, though traditionally in groups of three, have a long history in Japanese gardens, and an even longer one in China. They are symbolic of longevity, as are the carp on which live cranes feed. Dark matt grey is the classic colour for them.*

*RIGHT This classic basin, dipper and spout are in Koraku-en, one of the great tea gardens of Japan. Near Okayama, Koraku-en was started in 1687. Reached by a bridge from the castle of the Lord of Okayama, it has always been much admired, and was continually developed until 1863. Kuraku-en translates as 'after, ease' meaning the delights of the garden and gardening after a life as a politician and warrior.*

*ABOVE Even the smallest outdoor space can have a tiny pool of still water. In the past, every Chinese garden grew a plant of the sacred lotus, either in a pond, or in a ceramic container like this. It is a good way to grow any of the smaller half-hardy or tropical water lilies. The lotus is heavy with religious significance for Buddhists; others simply admire the leaves and the marvellous perfume of the flowers.*

Canals, *miroirs d'eau,* and pieces of still water of all sizes became the rage, especially if the terrain suited them. The marshy land around the palace at Versailles eventually sported the most extraordinary canal of all: it is huge. Some of the most enchanting ones are elsewhere, and often smaller. André Le Nôtre, the great French landscape gardener of the seventeenth century designed grand gardens at Vaux-le-Vicomte, in Seine-et-Marne, and Versailles, but he is also associated with the very much more romantic Château de Courances, near Fontainebleau.

The English copied the French, but soon preferred natural-seeming lakes, in which to reflect great houses, garden pavilions, or ruined castles. Neither they, nor their French counterparts, ever used the water for planting. It had cost them so dear that the whole surface had to glitter. This changed in the late nineteenth century, when European and American plant breeders started crossing tropical with hardy species of waterlily. Almost every gardener wanted a pool in which to grow the new marvels. We still do.

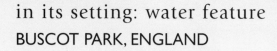

## in its setting: water feature
### BUSCOT PARK, ENGLAND

The great estate of Buscot Park, Oxfordshire, was well known in the eighteenth century for its extensive walled kitchen gardens and the landscape lakes created around 1775. Though grand, the 34 hectare (85 acre) garden acquired its most significant owner when the estate was bought in 1885 by the immensely successful banker Alexander Henderson, later Lord Faringdon.

In 1905, Lord Faringdon brought in the architect and garden designer Harold Peto. A leading expert on the Italian Renaissance, Peto made this extraordinary formal water garden to create a link between the great house and the main lake. The formal axis is 76m (250ft) long, and while the scheme does indeed have Renaissance elements, notably the series of splendid terms by the hedges, there are many other influences too. The way that the metre-high hedges of box separate the formal scheme from the forest beyond is as close in feel to the formal rides and allées of seventeenth-century France as it is to fifteenth-century Italy.

The manner in which narrow watercourses are linked to large rectangular pools would have been recognized in ancient Mesopotamia, and the complex shape of Buscot's main pool would have been familiar to gardeners in the Roman Empire, as well as those of Arab Spain. The charming little bridge could fit as easily over a Chinese canal in the city of Suzhou, as a canal in the back streets of Venice. However eclectic, the garden is full of style and mystery, and, as the water tumbles down through the sloping runnels, it sounds perfect too.

1 The flawless mirror of water, the fine stonework, grass, clipped hedges and the overarching forest make a perfect and serene picture. Entirely comparable scenes can be found in many seventeenth-century gardens in northern France. The theme of a mirror of water and enclosing greenery can make a strong design in much smaller spaces too.

2 The term, standing against the dark hedge, makes an exemplary contrast to the powerful horizontals that surround it. Its position demonstrates how a single feature, well placed, can bring vivid life to a scene. The central row of waterlilies will eventually cover the water surface and merely add to the greenery, but not to the magic.

3 Harold Peto's brilliant design makes use of the slope with a large-scale water staircase. The glimpse of the glittering waters of the lake make an end point to one of the most enticing pieces of formal gardening in England. The visitor is almost compelled to explore, and to find a way to the distant pavilion.

**4** Buscot's combination of large geometrically shaped pools, linked by a series of narrower channels is a piece of water design that ancient civilizations would have recognized. This type of design can also be scaled down to make an entrancing feature in gardens that are much less grand.

27

# PLANT SUPPORTS

# HOLDING UP THE CLIMBERS

There have been three big waves of development in the use of plant supports. In the ancient world, almost the only climbing plant in use was the grapevine. In addition to its fruit, the grapevine provided other great delights. The flower trusses have a faint but delicious perfume, and the translucent foliage gives a fine shade. Many gardens of the Roman Empire had pergolas draped with vines, and some of the courtyard houses of Pompeii had vines strung over the atrium. There were few other climbers to use. Native honeysuckles and European species of clematis such as *Clematis vitalba*, were joined by jasmines, early arrivals from China. Those plants constituted the entire range of medieval climbers.

It was the discovery of the Americas, and increasing trade with the East that set off the next great age of the climber. From the Americas came decorative and edible beans, squashes, bignonias, ipomoeas, and dozens of others. From the East, among many plants, came varieties of climbing rose, aristolochias, and different sorts of honeysuckle. As gardeners wanted to grow these new wonders the more affluent built trelliswork pavilions for them, while others filled their gardens with trellis obelisks and screens.

The third great age started at the end of the eighteenth century when the trickle of new species of rose that reached European gardens turned into a flood, and included more of American and Chinese climbing cultivars. Clematis species also became abundant, especially those from India and China. Once they were in the garden, the species crossed with abandon. Within quite a short period there were literally hundreds of glorious climbing roses and they became extremely popular. By the end of the nineteenth century, numerous varieties of clematis were available to gardeners too.

OVERLEAF *Stout ropes slung from the tops of poles make a perfect place for the luxuriant growth of the rose 'Rambling Rector', an old variety of unknown provenance. It does well when allowed to climb trees too and happily covers potting sheds and garages. It has light fragrance; use the related 'Seagull' if you want a stronger perfume.*

RIGHT *A scarlet-painted trellis obelisk makes a vivid feature among greenery, contrasting brilliantly with the yellow-green of the fennel flowers. Later in the season, a few strands of a dark red nasturtium would look good. Obelisks like this make the garden in winter exciting too.*

The modest rose arch and the brick-pillared pergolas of early twentieth-century gardens in Europe and America are both descendants of an ancient garden feature. Pergolas were common in every Roman garden, and whether simply built of olive or juniper poles, or more grandly of cedar and marble, they provided shade. They also yielded a crop of grapes. Even town houses had them: the House of the Centenary in Pompeii had a pergola with vines shading the courtyard's central pool. Sometimes, pergolas shaded other crops, and lemon trees and humble salad leaves flourished in the warm, dappled shade. Pergolas also shaded the summer dining areas of even the most modest house.

After the fall of the Roman Empire in AD 476 , pergolas remained a favoured way of growing domestic vines throughout medieval Europe. The first printed book on agriculture, *Opus Ruralium Commodorum* by Pietro de Crescenzi, appeared in several volumes around 1268–70. The eighth volume says that gardens should be filled with trellis arbours and pavilions. Many gardeners took up the ideas. One early example was Charles V's sumptuous and civilized gardens at the Hôtel Saint Pol in Paris, built between 1364 and 1380. It had many enclosures for orchards, vegetables and vineyards, each surrounded by trellis tunnels linking grander pavilions.

An Almerian poem of the fourteenth century describes a fine house and garden where the planting was ringed by an outer pergola of vines. In the sixteenth century, the

# CLASSIC PERGOLAS, TUNNELS & ARCHES

**RIGHT** *William Woodhouse designed this modern version of the nineteenth-century rose arch. It supports four wisteria plants, and when these have reached the top of the structure, the effect will be striking. Wisterias on small arches like this are much easier to prune than those on a large pergola.*

**CENTRE** *Handsome pergolas have a long tradition in Italy. Throughout the Roman Empire most gardens had a pergola to support vines. Here, at the Villa Carlotta on Lake Como, an early twentieth-century pergola supports oranges and lemons. Lemons reached Italy in the fourth century* AD, *oranges not until the late eleventh century.*

Tuscan country villas of the powerful Medici family had pergolas along ancient terraces that faced out over their vast domains. Gardens with a Persian influence, like Nishat Bagh in Kashmir, had water tanks and parterres of flowers interspersed with shaded pergolas, draped with jasmines and moonflowers.

Tunnels, pergolas and pavilions from the sixteenth to the early eighteenth century must have been well made. Many survived until the landscape movement of the 1730s overtook them and swept them away. In Scandinavia, the castle at Uppsala still had its pergolas in the mid-eighteenth century, and some pergola fragments remain at the castle of Tureholm in the Swedish province of Sodermanland, and date from about 1730. Gardeners were reluctant to see them go, and no wonder, for they were extremely attractive garden features. At Isola Bella, in northern Italy, for instance, where ten levels of garden descend to the waters of Lake Maggiore, the early eighteenth-century trellis work was once covered in a cascade of jasmine, pomegranates, oranges, and lemons. The present scheme of camellias and magnolias is much less glamorous, and dates from the mid-nineteenth century.

In the East, too, pergolas have been garden features from ancient times. In China, they often form galleries connecting the various buildings that compose the house and surround the garden. These covered ways were, and are, planned to give views of the garden or landscape. Light wooden pergolas were used for the display of the latest wisteria varieties, and still make one of the most delightful ways of showing off this glorious plant.

When, in the West, the landscape garden ideal began to collapse in the mid-nineteenth century, formal garden schemes came back into fashion, filled with brilliant

ABOVE *Apple trees have been used to make arbours since at least the sixteenth century, when their branches were twined together with honeysuckle and vine. Apple tunnels like this, fixed to wrought-iron arches, have been popular garden features since the early nineteenth century. These trees, at Toad Hall, Berkshire, are expertly pruned to keep the tunnel's shape and to crop well.*

bedding plants, sundials and urns. The faithful old pergolas and trellis pavilions were rather left out of the revival. While a number were built in the rustic style, popular in the 1870s and 1880s, using knotty woodland timber, the great new age of the pergola really started in the 1890s and continued until the First World War. Many gardens had pergolas with pillars of either brick, freestone, or fake Roman columns with roof timbers of oak.

At Hestercombe, in Somerset, Edwin Lutyens and Gertrude Jekyll designed a pergola that separates the flower garden from the countryside. The great industrialists Sir William Lever had the society designer Thomas Mawson plan a sumptuous Roman pergola at his town house, The Hill, Hampstead, in 1905. Abroad, English owners gave their gardens in the Giudecca at Venice, or in the Alps-Maritimes, pergolas draped with vine and rose. In North America, pergolas became the rage too; writer and designer Edith Wharton (1862–1937) made many. In modest British suburban gardens pergolas held pride of place, with roses like 'Greenfinch', and 'Paul's Scarlet Climber'.

The variety of arches and pergolas expanded too. There were laburnum tunnels, apple tunnels, and wisteria pergolas. In northern Europe, a series of metal arches was widely used for laburnum tunnels, using varieties like *Laburnum* 'Vossii', with flexible branches and long flower racemes. Fruit trees, too, were pruned over stout arches, or

*RIGHT  Gardeners of the western states of North America began to explore the riches of Japan rather than Europe from the late nineteenth century, and were vastly attracted to the numerous varieties of wisteria available there. This spectacular wisteria pavilion is in Saratoga, California and, with its Japanese-inspired balustrade and fine joinery work, makes a brilliant foil for the climber's flowers.*

formed into tunnels, pears and apples being the most biddable. In spring and autumn they can look particularly lovely.

Rose arches appeared in all styles and materials. Moorish or Gothic were common themes for wirework ones, often topped with turned wooden finials, once painted or gilded. Simple wrought-iron ones were also popular and can still be found in old gardens. Most common of all were arches of rustic wood seen in pre-war suburban gardens all over Europe and North America. Arches are still popular garden features, framing gateways or seats, or giving height to the flower border. They are used for displaying modern clematis hybrids, and some of the rambling and climbing roses that get less mildew on an arch than they do against a wall. The ravishing 'Blairii Number Two' is a good example.

A luxuriant mass of roses and clematis, a vine or a wisteria can be tremendously heavy, and offer considerable wind resistance. Pergolas and arches need to be strong, well anchored, and allow for tall visitors. That said, they make the loveliest garden features, and an early summer morning beneath their shade is a delight. They do not have to be fancy. The frames can be of sturdy rustic poles at intervals of 10m (33ft) inter-connected with simple wires. A good pergola offers a green privacy in overlooked gardens, and after dark, with tactful lighting, can be a lovely place, half room and half garden.

**LEFT** *For well over 2,000 years vine-covered dining areas, almost exactly like this, have been attached to Mediterranean cottages and farmhouses. During the Roman Empire the seating would have been a comfortable* triclinium, *but the feel is much the same. Glass lanterns make this twentieth-century version a pretty place at night.*

Some plant supports can give a garden planting a classic architectural feel too. Trellis obelisks can look good in the smallest garden, and give instant emphasis to the simplest flower bed. They have been an enjoyable feature of gardens great and small since the seventeenth century, but refer back to the monuments of ancient Egypt and ancient Rome. It was the re-erection of ancient stone obelisks in front of St Peter's in Rome in the early Renaissance that turned the obelisk into a symbol of the new interest·in the past. Topiary obelisks became a common feature in gardens. However, topiary needs

# PLANT-SWATHED OBELISKS & ROPES

*ABOVE These architectural plant pillars support an epiphytic flora of bromeliads, part of the collection of the Brazilian garden designer Roberto Burle Marx. In less tropical climes pillars like these can support a luxuriant flora if the plants are watered regularly.*

clipping, whereas a lightweight climber on a wooden frame looks as good during the growing season, and needs no work.

Obelisks made of wooden laths became the rage, and one grand series of trellis obelisks appeared in the Dutch gardens of Zorgvliet, a hunting lodge of William of Orange, who was an extremely keen gardener from the 1670s. Aided by his favourite, Hans Willem Bentinck, the garden was packed with incident: trellis obelisks and pavilions, topiary, and colourful ceramics from the Far East. Another of William's Dutch residences, Huis ten Bosch had trellis obelisks close in shape to the Egyptian originals, but shorter. It was not just aristocrats who could afford obelisks. Contemporary illustrations show modest houses with climber-swathed obelisks in beds of hollyhocks and myrtles.

When William and Mary ruled from London in the seventeenth century, Dutch fashion came to British gardens. In 1728, Batty Langley's extremely influential book, *New Principles of Gardening* was published. Although it shows the start of a movement for naturalistic gardening the book also advocates lawns decorated with wooden obelisks covered with passionflowers, honeysuckle, jasmine and grapes.

Batty Langley does not mention a popular flowering climber of the day, used in nosegays, and commonly found around garden houses and arbours: the scarlet bean. We know it as the runner bean. Introduced some time in the sixteenth century, it was

CENTRE *At Regent's Park in London a luxuriant planting of roses is garlanded along ropes. This mode of growing roses originated in a famous Regency garden near Slough, in Buckinghamshire, called Dropmore Lodge, owned by Lady Grenville, a famous gardener of the early nineteenth century.*

LEFT *A tiny stainless steel spiral obelisk supports a few leaves of an* Epimedium *hybrid, but it could just as easily support floppy annuals. Enlarged, it would create a splendidly modern reworking of the obelisks that first appeared in seventeenth-century Dutch gardens, and are still popular today.*

widely known by 1633, and must once have grown up much grander obelisks than the kitchen garden bamboo familiar today. It was hardly used as a table crop until the nineteenth century. In 1885, a major French seedsman's catalogue said: '. . . they are often trained over wire or woodwork, . . . to form summer houses or coverings for walks.' By then, obelisks, often of wirework, supported the grand new clematis hybrids developed by nurseryman George Jackman (1837–87).

In today's gardens, obelisks are enjoying a considerable revival, whether in old-fashioned wooden trellis painted in smart colours, or in wire mesh stretched over a metal framework, and topped off with an interesting finial. When painted they offer some exciting planting possibilities: indigo obelisks and bronze red nasturtiums, or yellow obelisks and green-blue passionflowers, even scarlet obelisks and white-flowered varieties of the old runner bean. Obelisks made from unbarked hazel and alder rods are more suitable for rustic gardens.

Until the late eighteenth century, the only common climbing rose was *Rosa moschata* with single and double forms. Every other type of rose was a bush, a few of which, like the lovely *Rosa alba* 'Plena' could be persuaded to grow to 2m (6ft 6in) high.

By the end of the eighteenth century, new introductions had improved the choice. While some of the new species like *Rosa filipes* from China, and *R. multiflora* from Korea and Japan, were almost as vigorous as lianas, others produced stems that rarely grew longer than 5m (16ft). These were crossed with bush varieties and produced hybrids that were pruned rather like raspberries, and needed pillars or poles to support them. Rose gardens were extremely popular and many had poles for these modestly clambering, and often very beautiful, plants.

**ABOVE** *Classic trellis obelisks, of the type once common in French and Dutch gardens well into the eighteenth century, are now enjoying a renaissance. This one is supporting a luxuriant growth of climbing squashes. In the past, obelisks like this were often used for some of the new species of climber that arrived from the Americas and the East in the seventeenth century.*

The less vigorous climbers developed at the end of the nineteenth century were grown up wooden posts too. These were often rustic, with bark and branch stubs left on. Tall, elaborate frames of metal strip were developed, which allowed rose stems to be twined more elegantly in and out. In very formal gardens, roses were tied to smart classical columns of wood and metal.

Once a garden had a sequence of rose-swathed poles, it was a simple step to sling a rope between their tops and this enabled more vigorous roses to be grown as well. The natural hang of the rope gave an elegant garland form to their growth. Some designers took up the idea with enthusiasm. At her Surrey house, Munstead Wood, Gertrude Jekyll had ropes slung from the oak balks supporting the loggia. The rose she used was a rampant beauty called 'The Garland', with huge clusters of soft amethyst-pink flowers that almost covered the glossy foliage.

Another celebrated designer, Harold Peto, slung ropes from poles making a screen on either side of a splendid Italianate pavilion at Bridge House, Weybridge, Surrey. Designed in 1906, the ropes were planted with *Parthenocissus henryana*, a good species to use because some of the stems hang elegantly downwards from their support. Gardeners in a hurry can use a fast-growing hop such as the golden-leafed *Humulus lupulus* 'Aureus,' for a similarly dramatic effect.

All these devices are clearly artificial. Some gardeners have always preferred to imitate nature, and let climbers scramble up living shrubs or trees. As a means of plant cultivation, the method has an ancient history too. In commercial production, the vineyards of ancient Rome had a number of ways of supporting the vines, one of the most picturesque being the use of peach trees as supports. The peach trees sometimes had ropes slung between them to give the vines more room. The variety of peach they used is still widely grown under the name *pêche de vignes*. Coming true from seed, it has fine yellow-skinned, aromatic and delicious fruit.

In northern Europe, orchard trees like apples and pears are usually too useful to be smothered by non-productive climbers. However, the writer Vita Sackville-West

ABOVE *The ultimate in the cottage garden ideal: an old sunlit orchard where the aging fruit trees support swags of flowering roses. It echoes the late Roman practice of growing vines through the branches of a peach tree, but the roses make harvesting the apples difficult. No matter; the final effect is wonderful. If too vigorous a rose is used, the tree will eventually be overwhelmed.*

popularized the pretty idea of growing roses up through their gnarled branches. It can look lovely, especially if the rose is planted at least 2m (6ft 6in) away from the tree's trunk, and the growing rose trained up into the crown of the tree. Good roses to use include vigorous varieties like 'Paul's Himalayan Musk', 'Seagull', and 'Bobbie James'.

Other exciting combinations are possible. The climbing hydrangea (*Hydrangea petiolaris*) looks wonderful sheathing trunks and branches of birch, and all the self-clinging vines, whether species of *Ampelopsis* (*A. megalophylla* can look stunning), or *Parthenocissus*, are worth using. Gardeners with warm gardens are fortunate, and can grow wonders like the trumpet vine (*Campsis radicans*), the subtropical passionflowers and hundreds of other types of climbing plants. Gardeners in colder climates can grow any of the many variants of the common ivy, and the genus *Clematis* is filled with a rich variety of magnificent beauties.

# THE DELICATE TRELLIS FRAME

**ABOVE** *This delightful screen, slightly Japanese in feel, but closer to a medieval European arbour in construction, is made of willow poles tied and bent to form the circular 'window'. Building it is easy, but for many gardeners obtaining the poles may be more difficult. Plant a few hazels, or a willow like* Salix alba, *coppice them, and in a few seasons you will have poles in abundance.*

Trellis is somehow redolent of gardens of the early decades of the twentieth century. It was then one of the universal features of gardens, along with beds of hybrid tea roses, a bird bath and a rockery. However, it has had an exciting and illustrious past and, today, offers tremendous potential to imaginative gardeners.

Trellis conjures up a structure made of neatly sawn wooden laths. But before the technology for such accurate cutting existed, garden structures were built with poles cut from coppices of alder, hazel, or willow. In the second part of *The Gardener's Labyrinth* (1577), Didymus Mountain described what he called a 'herber', a small kitchen garden arbour, made with juniper or willow poles, bound into a latticework with osiers (green and flexible willow thongs). It was covered with a planting of vines, melons, and cucumbers. Substitute bamboo stems for willow poles, and much of the huge variety of Japanese fences and garden screens can be thought of as trellis too. They are a world away from the stuffy orange-brown panels found in garden centres that contradict the notion that trelliswork has a place in stylish gardens.

For traditional trellises, various widths of wooden lath are easily available. Lath allows very formal designs, whether in the creation of flat architectural schemes for wall

decoration, or for three-dimensional architecture. Whatever its use, the planting should really be only a green and leafy decoration to the trelliswork, and should not be allowed to obscure its form and design. It is also helpful if the wood is painted or stained with a sympathetic colour rather than the usual wood-preservative brown.

Tunnels and arbours made of trelliswork are widely described and illustrated from the fifteenth century, but were probably common long before. They continued to grow in size and elaboration throughout the Renaissance, making galleries around knot-gardens or parterres, and even enclosing fountains, aviaries, and eating places. The owners of town houses wanted structures made of trellis too but, particularly in courtyards, there was hardly room for them. The solution was to apply trellis as flat panels to the walls. Seventeenth-century designers, like the Frenchman Daniel Marot, produced huge numbers of trellis designs that were widely copied not only in France, but also in Holland and Britain. William of Orange, who had a passion for trelliswork, commissioned Marot to work on his Dutch gardens, as well as on the gardens of Hampton Court.

In small spaces, the fanciful architectural panels were made with false perspective to suggest alcoves or vistas. They were put up in the hope that they would make a small yard feel more spacious. Perhaps they did. They were certainly most attractive, though none seem to have centred on mirrors, a feature that is currently popular.

Trelliswork was popular elsewhere in the garden, especially in the kitchen garden. In the early eighteenth century, kitchen garden walls were commonly covered in trellis, with vertical laths spaced 15cm (6in) apart, and the horizontals spaced at 20cm (8in). The branches of fruit trees were tied into the horizontals, and must have looked very lovely. Some gardeners already used taut wires, but most gardeners of the time did not think them as attractive as trellis. A descendant of fruit trellises can still sometimes be seen in nineteenth-century conservatories, where decorative trelliswork, often painted green, once supported peaches and nectarines.

However attractive, trellis has always had its critics. Even when the great seventeenth-century garden designer André Le Nôtre was designing trelliswork arbours and screens for Louis XIV, the grand Bishop of Avranches declared a dislike of '. . . the large broad sand-strewn allées, of trellises, parterres adorned only with a few delicate beds. . . edged with a few flowers and a few stunted trees. . .'. The critics regretted that the century preferred artifice to nature. The next century redressed the balance with the landscape revolution. However, not all trellis disappeared; it remained in French urban gardens where it can still be seen today.

With an increasing interest not only in old garden and craft techniques, but also countryside skills such as coppicing, gardeners of today are becoming interested in more informal trelliswork using the old materials like withies and hazel rods. In the best examples, the interplay between formal design and natural materials creates brand new classics. The new trellis makes perfect lightweight fences to half-screen a view, or to disguise a dull shed. It can be used to make airy arbours and pavilions, and in its classic way: against a wall, elegantly set off with strands of clematis, rose, or vine.

*CENTRE This sumptuous piece of trelliswork, made of copper strips riveted together, and designed by Julia Brett, is a thoroughly modern reworking of an ancient idea. Here, set against a plain white wall, and contrasted with a variety of Acer palmatum, it makes a very oriental picture.*

*ABOVE A piece of classic trellis panelling, typifies the mid-nineteenth century, at Nemours, Delaware, USA. Similar false perspectives and different grid sizes are found in trellis designs from the early seventeenth century. Though this one is not planted, these treillages once had a light decoration of passionflowers, hoyas or plumbagos.*

1 A potted lemon tree makes a handsome contrast with the formal arbour beyond, where the hornbeam almost entirely obscures the joinery of the arbour. William of Orange was a keen gardener, and collected many rare plants with which to decorate the garden.

2 This magnificent reconstruction of the main arbour in the Queen's Garden at Het Loo shows how this sort of garden feature must have looked in the seventeenth century. Such features were included in great gardens from the early Renaissance onwards. Some were more intensively architectural than this, with cornices and pilasters echoing Roman buildings. The central pavilion at Het Loo would once have contained seating and aviaries.

# in its setting: plant supports
## HET LOO, THE NETHERLANDS

When William of Orange and his English wife Mary became joint rulers of England in 1689 they left Holland to live in Britain. However, they so loved William's Dutch estate at Het Loo, and the memories of the quiet life they had once lived there, that they continued to develop its gardens although they lived in another country.

Today, visitors emerge from the shadowy vaults of the palace into a recreation of their astonishing garden, and may find it hard to believe that the enormous parterres, the obelisks of yew and juniper and the gilded statuary of the fountains, are all comparatively new, dating from 1975. Its most astonishing feature is the reconstruction

**3** A view through the tunnel; when the hornbeam covering is fully grown, the shading will be deeper, though if pruned annually the foliage will never block all the light. The timber framework at Het Loo is stained a tactful green, but in the sixteenth century, wooden garden structures like this were often brilliantly painted and gilded.

of the great arbours of the Queen's Garden. The original garden was well documented. When Mary returned to England, she never saw Het Loo again, but commissioned an exact account of the gardens as they were being built. This contained measurements of hedge heights and trellis work, lists of plants, and specifications for gravels and so on.

At Het Loo, the palatial arbours are made of wooden frameworks that support the flexible branches of hornbeams. Green tunnels and pavilions had been created in grand gardens all over Europe since at least the sixteenth century, and contemporary illustrations often show that grand arbours like this enclosed shady fountains, seats, and even aviaries, all designed to make them places of delight on a summer day. However, even modest gardens contained similar features, though fruit trees and scented climbers such as honeysuckle and jasmine would have replaced the more formal hornbeam.

43

# WALLS, GATES, PATHS & STEPS

# PROTECTING PARADISE

Gardens grow food crops and other plants important to the gardener. They have always needed protection from both animal and human marauders, and even the most ancient gardens of Mesopotamia were walled. The word for these gardens, defended, safe and beautiful, was *pairidaeza*, which reached the Greek language as *paradeisos* through Xenophon, the Greek essayist who first heard it in 401 BC. Descended directly from these ancient paradises, European gardens were walled, fenced, and even moated, well into the sixteenth century. For 200 years from the time of early settlements, all North American gardens, including those in the comparatively safe east, needed wooden palisades to protect them from native invaders, although when George Washington began to alter his inherited estate at Mount Vernon in 1787, he preferred his lawns only to be fenced by posts and chains.

Walls and gateways have always been among the garden's major design features. Even ancient paradises had decorated as well as defensive gateways, and gates and gateways still offer some of the most exciting and mysterious features that a garden can have. Some boundaries were given other sorts of openings from which to view the potentially dangerous world outside. Seventeenth-century gardens in northern Europe had *clairvoyées*, a dip in the height of a wall, or a 'window' , filled with a decorative grille for protection. Chinese gardens have a variety of lattice-work windows from which to view the world, or other aspects of the garden.

Paradise needs tending if it is not to become wilderness. Paths allow its cultivation, and help to reveal its beauty. At first purely functional, paths became decorative elements in the garden's design, sometimes reaching astonishing heights of visual sophistication. And as paradise is not always flat, the gardener has needed steps not only to accommodate its changes in level, but also to give some areas special emphasis.

OVERLEAF  *A simple American post-and-rail fence echoes the planking*
*of the house, beneath a magnificent Cornus specimen.*
*The rails are nailed to the posts, although older examples often have*
*rails that taper at the end, and fit into rough-cut sockets in the posts*
*to allow easy replacement of broken or rotten timbers.*

RIGHT  *Wall openings that give a view of the outside world have*
*been used since the seventeenth century. This one is in the late*
*nineteenth-century garden at Polesden Lacey in Surrey.*
*Though made in classic English flint and brick, it borrows its*
*attractive shape from Chinese gardens.*

The construction of walls can reveal much about the owner's personality and standing. Walls can express the power and prestige of great landowners, or the modest lifestyles of humble cottagers. They can give a garden a sense of theatre and surprise, or a background to show off the beauties of the plants. Walls can be used to link the garden to the outside world, as well as make the division even more powerful.

Even when, in eighteenth-century Europe, walls fell from fashion during the great landscape movement, they did not vanish. The invention of the ha-ha merely meant that

# THE GARDEN'S BOUNDARIES

the walls were sunk for their full height into a trench in the lawn. The ha-ha was invisible from the house, but daunting to beasts or men beyond the pale. Present-day suburban North America sees walls as undemocratic, and consequently its front gardens are without boundaries. European suburbs follow suit. Yet walls and boundaries offer many design and planting possibilities, and can be very imaginative.

The moat, possibly the most romantic of all garden enclosures, was reserved for landowners. A number of medieval moated pleasances survive (there is a splendid example at Kenilworth in Warwickshire). They were still being made in 1618 when the writer William Lawson suggested it was a slight matter to enclose the garden with a moat, further protected with a quickthorn hedge on the inner bank. The bank itself was to be '. . . level on the top two yards, broad for a fair walk, five and six foot higher than the soil, with a gutter on either side, two yards wide and four feet deep, set without with three or four chefs of thorns, and within with Cherries, Plums, Damsons, Bullis, and Filbirds.'

However delightful that must have been, in most garden cultures gardeners have found it simpler to accept the inevitability of ordinary walls, and to adapt them as design features in the garden. They can be very exciting. In small gardens, they can certainly be a dominating feature, needing careful treatment to make them less overwhelming. Made of simple materials used in a decorative way, or decorated with intriguing surfaces, they can offer great delight. Alternatively, they can be given unusual shapes, or covered with climbing plants, or even become places on which to grow a rich diversity of flowers.

Apart from enclosing the garden, and giving it security and privacy, garden walls can be used to divide the garden into areas, most usually separating functional elements like sheds, compost heaps and vegetable beds, from the show garden. There too, walls

**ABOVE** *Concrete lends itself perfectly to cool classic walls like these in the Jardin des Fournials, France. Unplanted and warmly coloured, they make a dramatic frame to the traditional joinery gate beyond and entice exploration of what is beyond.*

can be used as features in their own right, rather like theatre scenery flats, and can make a small space seem larger by offering an invitation to explore mysterious, concealed regions of the garden. Walls can even become invisible, supporting drifts of climbers, or fans or espaliers of delicious fruits. Or they can be used as they are in China, where walls create a background for plants and their shadows made by either the sun, the moon, or lantern light. The whitened walls of the smallest courtyards are used to display camellias and bamboos to perfection. Western gardeners should copy the idea more often.

Gardeners worldwide have long used living plants to make garden boundaries and divisions. Stock-proof quickthorn hedges were commonly used in Europe from at least Roman times, and probably much earlier. More formal hedges were made of the flexible stems of hawthorn and hazel woven together. In the West, also since Roman

**BELOW** *The Brazilian landscape and garden designer Roberto Burle Marx (1909–1994) assembled this dramatic garden wall from fragments of buildings that were being demolished in Rio de Janeiro. Dramatic foliage and stonework make an exceptionally exciting garden, which was created during the 1970s and 1980s.*

**BELOW** *Cloud walls, sometimes known as dragon walls, like this one at the Yuyan garden, Shanghai, were used in Chinese gardens to make a connection between views of the sky and the garden. The base of the wall is stonework, the rest of mud and straw. The dragon's scales, made of tiles, protect it from rain.*

times, garden hedges have sometimes been given topiary flourishes such as castellations or rows of clipped globes. Japanese gardeners have used native bamboos to make impenetrable barriers, but with great visual refinement. In some, carefully woven and tied living bamboo stems are intertwined with wisteria.

Wood has always been the simplest material for garden boundaries. It has been used in pointed balks to make the defensive palisades so often seen in medieval illustration; in split chestnut poles to make simple palings, or the simple post-and-rail fences familiar throughout North America. There, too, can be found the modest picket fences, sometimes with lightly decorated main posts. On the other side of the world, bamboo poles and laths, or bunches of twigs bound with rope or string, make lovely Japanese garden fences. These are often tall where they face the street, and low when they divide a tea garden from the main area, or form decorative screens called sleeve fences.

Wood eventually decays. Bricks can last for thousands of years, and in the West, they have been used for garden walls at least since Roman times. They remained popular well into the nineteenth century, for urban gardens, as well as for country ones, and especially for the inner surface of kitchen garden walls. Brick retains the heat of the sun well, and brick surfaces were esteemed backings for espalier fruit trees, especially varieties that needed cossetting to produce either an early crop, or any crop at all. Experiments to find which sort of fruit did best on what height and aspect of wall were in full swing by the seventeenth century.

However, brick walls of any height need several thicknesses of bricks to make them stable. The only way round the problem was to build the curving crinkum-crankum walls sometimes found in eighteenth- and early nineteenth-century gardens, though sadly hardly used in modern ones. Though only a single brick thick, the curves gave them considerable stability, and many still survive. Some were used as fruit walls; Thomas Jefferson had one in his garden at Monticello in Virginia USA.

Stone is mostly immortal, whether humble flint or finest marble. It is also valuable, and can easily be recycled, sometimes to the dismay of archaeologists, but often to the considerable benefit of the garden. Most stone walls have a core of rubble, and once the mortar that holds the wall together weathers, vegetation can grow in it. Using the garden wall as a vertical rockery has a classic history too, the sixteenth-century herbalist John Gerard grew *Corydalis claviculata* (his 'white fumiterre') and *Corydalis lutea* 'his 'yellow fumiterre') on walls in his London garden. The yellow fumitory remained

**BELOW** *A classic picket fence is basically the same as the post-and-rail fence, but with vertical laths nailed along the rails. They were common in eighteenth-century town gardens in Britain and America, and always painted white, which led to complaints from contemporary stylists as they regarded white as being rather loud and suburban.*

popular. Philip Miller, in charge of the Chelsea Physic Garden, in London, from 1722 to 1770, wrote in *The Gardeners Dictionary*, that many plants, liking 'morter', did well 'upon old Walls or Buildings, to hide their Deformity'. Indeed, some plants, like the wallflower, take their name from their delight in growing there, but valerian, toadflax, cotyledon, and many others can look as attractive. In tropical gardens, bromelias and orchids are easily encouraged to decorate walls.

But gardeners till the soil, and its basic mud has been used to make some of the most perfect garden walls of all. Cob, a mix of mud and straw, was recommended by William Lawson. In his delightful book *A New Orchard and Garden*, (1618) he writes that such walls should be heavily 'plaistered' with wallflowers so that bees could use it for honey. In China, the extraordinary cloud walls are made of a similar mix, although rubbed with chalk to whiten the surface. In some, the chalk is oiled and buffed to make it shine like marble, while the top is protected by dark, glazed tiles that are supposed to imitate the celestial dragon's scales.

Modern classics are almost all built of concrete, and, free of the past, most imaginative new garden walls are from the Americas. American designers use concrete with tremendous visual flair. Screens, baffles, entrances and stairs are sometimes gloriously and daringly coloured, and often brilliantly contrasted with their plantings. European gardeners should take note.

# GATES & GATEWAYS

**ABOVE** *Even in walled kitchen gardens, the gate could be given a mild architectural flourish, as in the arched top of this one. In the seventeenth and eighteenth centuries it was common to give them a luxuriant surround of flowers. Although bereft of them, this old gate has great allure.*

**LEFT** *This witty modern garden gate is built from old garden implements, an allusion to eighteenth-century plasterwork trophies found on some country house walls or ceilings. The wooden fence has a classic eighteenth-century chinoiserie pattern, and the gate centres on a curiously proportioned obelisk – a modern take on a thoroughly classical idea.*

Even the most ardent gardener would not want to be forever walled up in paradise. Walls (and other boundaries) need gates. The ancient walled paradises of Persia had gateways that were both fortified and often splendidly decorated too, a tradition that lasted for thousands of years. When Ruy Conzales de Clavijo, ambassador of the King of Castille and Leon, visited Samarkand, Uzbekistan, in 1402 for the wedding of six sons of Tamerlane, the Mongol conqueror, he wrote 'Attendants took charge of us . . . and led us forward, entering the orchard by a wide and very high gateway, most beautifully ornamented'. Samarkand's many gateways, some which Clavijo will have seen, are still covered in wonderful and complex patterns of brilliant blue tiles. Many other ancient Middle Eastern and Kashmiri gardens still show an array of battlemented walls and lofty gateways.

Garden gateways have always had a ceremonial function, and even though that is often very modest, they are an important feature in any garden lucky enough to have them. They can be used to frame views of distant garden paths, or another garden feature, such as a pavilion or an urn. If the gate is solid, and closed, they can offer an almost irresistible mystery; a garden gate can almost demand that the passer-by peers through a chink, or a grille set into peeling woodwork.

Good gates, and gateways too, can augment the visual style of the garden. Rustic gates suggest cottage gardens buzzing with bees. Wrought-iron gates, covered in flowers and leaves, and painted in appropriate colours can suggest calm and silence. Some European gardens have gates on walls, which are entirely false, and lead nowhere. Gates like that can make a strong visual focus in the garden, with a mystery of their own.

*ABOVE Wallflowers, old brick walls, and a slightly squint gate of old pieces of batten nailed to a simple 'Z' framework make a classic, and very nostalgic, garden view. The low wall was called a 'breast wall' in the eighteenth century, and is the most common height of wall for cottage gardens.*

In the West, gateways are most often simple rectangular openings, sometimes arched, and sometimes given an architectural frame. That is conservative. In Chinese gardens, gateways can be found in dozens of shapes, the most celebrated being the circular moon gate. These, set into plain walls, and often emphasized by a short flight of steps, create dramatic views of the garden that lies beyond them. Though European missionaries and traders visited Chinese gardens from the seventeenth century onwards, moon gates became well known only in the late nineteenth century when they became very popular with Western gardeners.

Gates and gateways certainly offer themselves as tremendous planting opportunities. In northern Europe in the seventeenth and eighteenth centuries, the wall on either side of a humble kitchen garden gate was given special treatment and left clear of espalier fruit. The space was for a generous planting of jasmines, honeysuckles and roses. It is still a splendid combination, but very cold gardens need *Jasminum* × *stephanense* rather than the less hardy but very much more perfumed *Jasminum officinale*.

Wooden gates display all sorts of local traditions. One Dutch print of 1659 shows a lovely old country house, with gardens of orchards, green tunnels, and hedges. The wooden railings and gates are boldly painted with stripes and lozenges that were common 400 years earlier. Parsonages and cottages in remote parts of Norway still have gates with decorative cut-out patterns. The simple gate made of wooden palings is one of the great classics of the kitchen garden, while the sun-burst gate is a classic of 1930s suburban European gardens. Today, the colour of the gate can contrast with the planting;

RIGHT *Typical of eighteenth-century European wrought-iron gates, this handsome example is ornamented generously with repoussé foliage,and now set into a fine brick wall at the Filioli gardens in California. These gates, always symbols of wealth, were once painted intense blues or greens, and often highlighted with gold leaf. The heavy framework gives the gate a great sense of solidity and weight, which is often missing in modern examples.*

RIGHT *Many Chinese gardens have circular moon gates. This one, framed in stone and set in a plain wall, is emphasized by steps leading up to and beyond it. Now that the gateway no longer needs to protect and exclude, openings like this are designed to create startling changes of light and shade, and dramatic garden views.*

try an indigo-blue gate in an ivy-covered wall, or a scarlet gate in a wall draped with a self-clinging vine like *Pathenocissus quinquefolia* or *Pathenocissus henryii*. Basal plantings are important too, and narrow-leafed plants like daylilies (*Hemerocallis* species and varieties), or clumps of Japanese anemones, or even the huge architectural leaves of *Acanthus mollis*, can give exciting emphasis to the simplest gate.

Metal gates are much grander, and great buildings have had gates of bronze and gold since ancient Rome. Iron gates have been common in gardens since at least the sixteenth century. They were often simple ranks of bars with arrow or spearhead tops. The great age of the decorative metal gate, all flourishing foliage, heraldic devices, and

flowers, was the seventeenth century, and these gates have remained a feature in the gardens of the wealthy ever since. Now, most are painted black, though that was not their original colour; many were painted intense blue, dark green, or Indian red, enlivened with as much gilding as the owner could afford. Modern wrought-iron gates are often too lightweight in both substance and imagination, but those made by craftsmen and women can be expensive. Nevertheless, some imaginative garden gates are made today, using all sorts of modern alloys. The American architectural historian Charles Jencks commissioned some innovative garden gates in unusual shapes and a variety of materials including polished stone and stainless steel, with inscribed mottoes, for his garden near Dumfries in Scotland.

In fourteenth-century Moorish Spain, the garden of the Alcazar in Seville had garden paths that were built upon vaulted supports 3m (10ft) high, making them level with the tops of a grove of orange trees. Visitors could stroll through a carpet of scented orange flowers. Most garden paths are far more modest, being merely ways of getting from one part of a garden to another without getting muddy.

The most common hard-path surface in modern gardens is probably gravel. River gravel, especially a fine grade like pea gravel, gives a more sympathetic surface than stone

# PATHWAYS & PAVING

chippings. In eighteenth-century Britain, the most sought after was gravel from London's Kensington, which was a biscuit colour that looked well against grass and flowers. Unlike too many modern paths, which consist of small stones only, the gravel was mixed with a quarter of its weight in sand and set on a foundation of larger stones, then rolled until well consolidated. It still drained easily, but did not move constantly when used, let alone make the crunching noise so familiar in gravel paths today. Where the cost of transportation made the gravel too expensive, crushed shell was used as an alternative.

Nowadays, it is rare to find gravel used well. Too often it carpets an ugly area used for parking cars, though the late English garden designer John Codrington allowed parking areas to fade into the planting. Many of the plants he liked, especially aquilegias, *Alchemilla mollis*, and many geranium species, have seeds that germinate with gusto in

*LEFT  Wooden decking makes a comfortable lounging area suspended over the sloping margins of a pool, and creates a simpler entry down the steps. It also gives a smooth, though natural, contrast to the freestone crazy-paving pathway. The crevices between the stone need mowing when the plant growth becomes too luxuriant.*

*RIGHT  The narrow Shropshire town garden belonging to Mirabel Osler is both cottagey and classic. The garden writer has made use of luscious plantings, steps, arches and low walls to give it mystery. A herringbone brick path runs the whole length and unifies the various parts. Here, a sitting area is paved with old terracotta tiles, and cluttered with pots.*

gravel, and grow well, producing a most attractive effect. Fine gravels are sometimes used for paths in Eastern gardens too. The paths may symbolize water, and are meant to be looked at, rather than trodden upon. The Zen gravel gardens in Japan use coarser gravel as the main element, which is raked and left still, as a scene upon which to meditate.

One modern classic is made of wood. Decking is often over-used, but it is best for creating level spaces in a sloping garden, as it is far cheaper than making terraces, and it does not alter the basic land form. It can also be used to make walkways through, or even over, vegetation. Good examples are far more commonly seen in American, rather than European, gardens. Where timber is plentiful and cheap, decking can make an exciting feature. It warms and dries quickly after bad weather and is rarely damaged by extreme cold. In areas with severe winters, frost heave can ruin paved paths and patios, but decking makes a fine alternative.

In more temperate climates, the simplest of bricks can make marvellous garden paths and seating areas, especially when used in decorative patterns. When bricks are used as paving they can be combined into simple weave patterns, such as herringbone, or patterns inspired by the imagination of the gardener. Antique brick, rubbed and worn, looks best, though some can flake badly after frosts. Nineteenth-century glazed stableyard bricks look magnificent, but can be as expensive as antique bricks. If only modern materials are available, engineering grade brick is the best sort to use, and comes in reasonably sympathetic garden colours. Very dark tones can look exceptional.

Gardeners can sometimes get hold of nineteenth-century cobbles. These are wonderful things, their upper surfaces polished from use, and in good colours. In nineteenth-century boulevards and squares they were often laid in elaborate fan patterns, which are well worth trying to duplicate in the garden. Even better are the whinstone fragments chipped away when making the street cobbles. These fragments, 15cm (6in) long, were often hammered close together into a sand base to form pavements, and now make enviable garden paths.

Dressed stone, whether sandstone, limestone, slate, or granite, has always been used for the most luxurious paths. Sandstone is porous, and holds water within its bulk. That is perfect for growing moss, but can also make sandstone paving extremely slippery in winter. Slate, such as dark grey Caithness slate, is impermeable, so does not get a

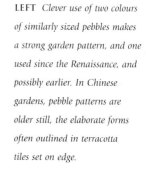

mossy, aged look. In nineteenth-century-gardens, slate yards and paths were regularly washed with linseed oil, which makes them look unpleasantly like sheets of toffee. Any gardener fortunate enough to be able to buy an old set of stone or slate paving stones to re-assemble in their garden, will need to map and number the stones. When originally cut, they were planned and numbered before delivery.

*BELOW Classic crazy paving requires great skill in fitting the stones together, plus masonry skills to shape recalcitrant pieces. Here, there is little space between the units. In some Japanese gardens, the junctions are filled with thin bands of pebbles, which saves stonework, but adds to construction time. It can look exceptionally handsome.*

A more informal look can be made by using freestone paving, which is irregular in plan, but has one flat surface. Freestone paving looks good in informal gardens, and plants colonize the gaps between the stones easily. Crazy paving is a self-conscious variant of freestone paving and good examples are made of stone. It was first popular in the late nineteenth century, when there was a vogue for things Japanese. A refined version was used for paths to tea houses. If stone is too expensive, consider a different surface, as crazy paving made with broken concrete slabs is 'classic' in only one way.

The greatest feat in imaginative path and patio building lies in the successful use of mixed materials, whether two or three colours of pebble, brick and stone, or cobble and gravel. Mixing is a good way of making use of small quantities of several materials, and can produce some extremely elegant results. Mixed material paths have been used in Chinese gardens for at least 1,000 years. The design framework was sometimes of tiles set on end, infilled with elegantly laid pebbles.

Part of their attraction comes from the use of the simplest and cheapest of materials in a way that produces a sumptuous and expensive effect. Much simpler paths can be made by using a grey river-washed gravel divided into squares by rows of black whinstone cobbles. Brick margins around flagstones, or old paving stones can look excellent, and even concrete slabs can look much livelier if relieved by rows of brick dividers.

Many sorts of seeds find that the interstices between flagstones or bricks offer perfect places for germination. In informal spaces, a few verbascums or alchemillas can look enchanting, but dandelions and thistles like paving too. Tree and shrub seedlings are even more of a nuisance. Careful hand-spraying with a systemic weedkiller is the answer, and will kill the taproots of Welsh poppies and other weeds which are impossible to remove with a trowel. The usual weedkillers damage mosses and lichens too, so a too widespread use of them will stop the paths or terraces ever getting the patina of age. Some flowers amongst the cracks can look enchanting: *Dianthus* 'Loveliness' has a marvellous perfume, *Erigeron karvinskianus* does not, but is too pretty to resist. Neither grows large enough to trip up the gardener during a midnight stroll. However, formal garden areas and gravel or pebble paths always look best with no plants at all.

**RIGHT** *Broad and deep grass steps like these, at Misarden Park, Gloucestershire, are generous and leisured, and a serious invitation to a barefoot stroll after dark as the dew settles. The steps have low retaining walls of the same stone that flanks them. Grass would soon colonize the walls, though here flowers are planted along each step, which must make for complicated mowing. Steps like these would also work wonderfully winding upwards through a hillside orchard.*

# STEPPING UP IN THE GARDEN

A sloping garden can cause some gardeners concern, yet in spite of the expense and difficulty of building steps, they can easily be one of the most exciting features in the garden, giving wonderful planting opportunities and plenty of visual drama. Steps should be used whenever moving about the garden becomes a scramble rather than a gentle amble. Steps are subtle things, and can give an almost imperceptible, but nevertheless significant, emphasis to a particular part of the garden. Even a single step up on to a terrace or lawn, or down to a pool garden can make the area special.

Steps have always been used to give ceremonial status to particular areas, whether a seating dais, or the *cour d'honneur* of French castles and manor houses. They are sometimes only raised by one step, yet they mark the barrier to social inferiors with perfect clarity. In the garden, steps create visual emphasis for centrepieces and other focal points, and can even play with the design and shape of the garden. In some Italian gardens flights of steps narrow as they ascend, so altering the perceived perspective of the view. The steps themselves can be decorated. At the late seventeenth-century Villa Barbarigo, stone steps leading up to a private garden even have verses carved on them, describing the garden as a private paradise where 'Sun and moon shine brightly, Mars lays down his weapons, Death is powerless and tears have no place'.

Stone, of course, is the great classic material for steps, while marble is used for palatial types, cut blocks of sandstone and limestone for middling ones, and random freestone for the simplest or the most informal. Freestone is the most fun to use, though the leading edge of a step needs to be made of the biggest stones, and cemented as

**LEFT** *Steps based on Japanese models, can be found in many late nineteenth-century European rock gardens. A good example, where the masonry is also as skilfully and expensively done is at Cragside, in Northumberland. The invitation to explore up the steps through the tunnel of misty greenery is irresistible.*

**ABOVE** *Wooden steps and decking form the backbone of this steeply sloping urban garden. Designed by Chris Jacobsen, the eight steps are an invitation to the seating area and beyond. The luxuriant planting increases the excitement and allure.*

**LEFT** *Informal freestone steps, from the Lutyens-Jekyll partnership, at Hestercombe in Somerset, make a gentle and generous arc, and are designed to allow plants to seed themselves into the cracks. The effect is pretty and easy to achieve, though not suited to heavy use, or a mad dash for the phone.*

securely as possible. Many shapes become possible, whether simple curving flights of steps up the slope, or the handsome semi-circular flights of shallow steps long beloved by gardeners. There is a fine seventeenth-century example at Brécy, in Normandy. The architect Sir Charles Barry designed a long flight of them for Trentham Hall, in Staffordshire, in 1833, but they are now mostly associated with gardens designed by Edwardian architect Edwin Lutyens, and his gardener friend Gertrude Jekyll.

Brick, too, can make classic steps, though heavy wear loosens bricks on the leading edge of each step, and they need occasional maintenance. However, the look can be a delight. In country or ecological gardens, where bricks might be out of place, timber can make extremely attractive steps. They can be made of balks of timber securely pegged to the front of each step, or in deck planking to link a deck to garden proper.

Timber balks, or low, freestone retaining walls, allow grass treads for steps, which looks enchanting, but difficult to mow. They can be, however, one of the great delights in the garden. Over the centuries, grass steps have been used to make places to sit too. The medieval jousting yard at Dartington Hall, in Devon, has grass steps from which to view the contests. In preference to violent armoured warriors, many eighteenth-century Italian country houses have green theatres for viewing harlequinades, or more serious drama. Grass steps have also been popular on the other side of the Atlantic: there is a pretty late eighteenth-century flight at the Moffat-Ladd garden in New Hampshire.

Steps of all sorts offer immensely exciting planting possibilities, especially if the plants are scented. In fourteenth-century Moorish Spain, flights of steps often ascended through thickets of perfumed Persian lilac (*Syringa persica*). Early in the season, great masses of the slightly floppy daylily (*Hemerocallis lilioasphodelus*), grown in Europe since the sixteenth century, will fill the air with its scent, and roses can take over once it is finished. A tiny violet like *Viola labradorica* colonizes steps with abandon, though forms of the perfumed *Viola odorata* are almost as vigorous.

**RIGHT** *The Giardino Giusti in Verona shows that flights of steps can be sinister as well as ceremonial. Here, between the dark cypresses, they narrow in stages to dramatize the perspective, and could almost lead the way to the Underworld, a feeling enhanced by the gap-toothed giant higher up the hill. In fact, the dark archway leads to what was once a grotto decorated with shells and mirrors.*

**1** The same patterns of blocks form retaining walls, terraces and house. Linear leaves always work well against formal walls, and irises, libertias, daylilies, and phormiums should all be used in such plantings.

**2** These powerfully moulded and shadowed blocks make a wonderful contrast and backing to the water and the waterlilies. Too many pools are set into flat yards; if backed by a wall they can be far more dramatic, and give splendid opportunities for planting.

## in its setting: walls
# STORER HOUSE, LOS ANGELES, USA

**3** A corner of the house shows how terraces, walls, paths, steps, and planting have been integrated to make a dazzling whole. Here, sections of wall have been left clear of plants, and become places for the dramatic shadows of plants instead.

**4** Plain blocks, used for sections of the wall of the house, are also used for terrace surfaces and paths. In the main paths, the outer two rows of blocks are half the width of the rest. This fine detail makes the edging clear and sharp in an ingenious and subtle way.

Almost the apotheosis of concrete, this glorious house was designed by the architect Frank Lloyd Wright in 1923, for Dr John Storer. Constructed with what Lloyd Wright called his 'textile' blocks, made of precast patterned concrete and strengthened with an internal system of steel bars, the walls of the house are as richly textured as the garden. Set into a steep hillside, the architect ensured that the building was closely integrated into its dramatic site by using a series of walls and terraces that reach out into and re-order the landscape. The exciting form and textures of the blocks, and the intense shadows and generous plantings enable the gardens, house, and landscape to work together in a way that makes this one of the architect's masterpieces.

The terraces and steps to the front have full views of Hollywood, Los Angeles, and the San Bernardino Valley. The private side of the house looks on to a courtyard garden, half sunk into the rising hillside. Where space allows, paths and terraces of chamfered blocks are merged into the greenery by using the same blocks as stepping stones into grass. The place is absolutely modern in its massing, but partly Mayan, partly Mycenaean in feel. It is an inspiration to many gardeners to have somewhere as exciting to plant.

Frank Lloyd Wright wrote of The Storer House: 'Classical architecture was all fixation; . . . now . . . let walls, ceiling, floors become seen as component parts of each other, their surfaces flowing into each other'. The architect could easily have added 'gardens' too.

# TOPIARY, KNOTS & MAZES

# THE ANCIENT ART OF TOPIARY

Many garden cultures shear plants into artificial forms. In the East, Japanese gardeners shape and prune to intensify the natural form of bushes and trees. Topiary is also an ancient tradition in the West. Contemporary accounts of Roman Empire gardens show that topiary was immensely popular. Pliny the Younger (AD *c*62– *c*113), an early garden writer, filled his Tuscan garden with figures and heraldic devices of clipped box.

The first modern European treatise on topiary appeared in 1300. It was illustrated with many shapes still found in today's gardens, and was widely read. Paintings of late medieval gardens commonly show topiaried plants. By the fifteenth century, Italian gardens competed for the number and ingenuity of their topiaries. The Rucellai garden at Quaracchi in Florence had a dazzling display which included topiaried temples, warriors, popes, cardinals, apes and donkeys. The rival Medici gardens had even more. Many gardens were as ornate for the next 200 years, though stylish gardeners used a few simple and beautiful shapes, notably narrow obelisks and simple globes of green. Topiary was frowned on during the landscape movement of the eighteenth century, and only a few English and French examples survived until there was a revival of interest in the late nineteenth century. Topiary then became associated with cottages rather than country houses.

Though Pliny used box, yew has been the classic topiary plant since the Renaissance. Its dense foliage clips to a magnificently smooth, dark green surface, and the branch structure is strong enough to make large and complex shapes. Privet, holly, phillyrea and bay are also classic topiary plants. The fast growing *Lonicera nitida* has been used only since 1908. All topiary takes time and effort to make and maintain, but a garden with one or many mature topiaries has a magic that almost no other garden feature can give it.

OVERLEAF *Ham House, near Richmond, Surrey, has a garden first planned in the 1670s by the Duke and Duchess of Lauderdale. Recently recreated in seventeenth-century style, dapper topiary cones and margins of box enclose flat-trimmed beds of white santolina and grey lavender to make a subtly coloured pattern. Surrounded by hornbeam arbours, the garden is an enchanting place.*

RIGHT *In Williamsburg, Virginia, this replica of an eighteenth-century American garden has a topiary in the estrade, or tiered, form that would have been familiar to many medieval gardeners. Here, it deftly echoes the gable of the house beyond the classic picket fence.*

Though the gardeners of the Roman Empire planted elaborate patterns of low, clipped hedges, there is little evidence that they looked like knots or strap work. However, those of early Renaissance gardens certainly did and one of the first printed books, *Hypnerotomachia Poliphili*, written by Francesco Colonna in 1464, is the richest source of early Renaissance garden imagery known to us. Knot gardens are among the features he describes in detail in this remarkable book.

# DECORATIVE KNOT GARDENS

A 'knot' is an elaborate, formal, and often complex pattern carried out with low growing plants kept neatly sheared into miniature hedges. The weave of the pattern is so dense that there is no room for any plants that are not part of it, and any spaces in between the hedges are usually filled in with gravel or sand. Knots need to be seen from a vantage point well above them, so they were usually planted near the house or summerhouse. Plants used to make the patterns included thymes, thrifts, and even double daisies. These were interwoven with larger plants such as the silver-leafed santolinas, or green box, which were all kept tightly trimmed so that they did not interfere with the line of the pattern. The different foliage colours allowed the viewer's eye to unravel the complexity of the knot.

**FAR LEFT** *The ancient, moated Helmingham Hall at Stowmarket in Suffolk has this delightful box parterre. The design is planted with old-fashioned flowers and herbs. There are various sorts of sage, helichrysums, and the sixteenth-century white form of the rose campion (Lychnis coronaria 'Alba')*

**LEFT** *Rosemary Verey's replica of a knot design at Barnsley House, Gloucestershire, is taken from Richard Surflet's 1583 translation of* La Maison Rustique *by Estienne and Liebault. It is made with box, wall germander (Teucrium chamaedrys), thymes and santolina. In the sixteenth century, designs like this were commonly used as one quarter of a larger square design.*

Knots were extremely popular, and must have been pretty. In Britain, good patterns were published in the first part (1571) of *The Gardener's Labyrinth* supposedly by Didymus Mountain, but in fact written by Thomas Hill. The book, written in two parts, 1571 and 1577, was a success and went through many editions. However, many garden knot designs were also taken from embroidery or marquetry pattern books of the period.

*Sir Thomas Hanmer's Garden Book*, written in 1659, but only published in the last century, notes that 'In these days the borders [of the garden] are not hedged about with privet, rosemary or other such herbs which hide the view and prospect . . . but all is commonly near the house laid open and exposed to the sight of the rooms and chambers, and the knots and borders are upheld only with very low coloured boards or stone, or tile'. However delightful, when Sir Thomas wrote, garden fashion was already changing. The tight regulation of the knots hardly allowed for the cultivation of the vast numbers of new flowering plants that were pouring into Europe from the Americas, the Middle East and the Orient, and so a rather different form of gardening had begun to appear in mainland Europe.

**ABOVE** *An exciting, contemporary way of putting ancient topiary features together is seen in this garden where classic balls and cones of yew stand on immaculate gravel, all enclosed in a sweeping hedge of box.*

# FORMAL PARTERRES & CLIPPED TOPIARY

The economic expansion of the sixteenth century led to the accumulation, for the fortunate, of great wealth. This, together with the new varieties of flowers that arrived in Europe meant that knot gardens were too tight and circumscribed for the new age that dawned with the seventeenth century. Starting in France, knot work began to loosen, becoming patterns of quite substantial box-edged beds, still set out in decorative patterns, but filled with the new flowers, particularly lovely bulbs like fritillaries, striped tulips, together with pinks, pulmonarias, bloodroots and many other new plants.

By 1650 knot gardens began to vanish altogether, leaving behind vast expanses of grass cut into grand scroll-work designs. Curiously, French gardeners called this feature in the garden *broderie anglaise*. However, English gardeners used a French word. Sir Thomas Hanmer wrote: 'If the ground be spacious, the next adjacent quarters or *parterres*, as the French call them, are often of fine turf, but as low as any green to bowl

**ABOVE** *The huge grass parterre at Kirby Hall, Northamptonshire, is entirely French in appearance, and is a recreation of the garden's glory in the seventeenth century. It is likely that the containers would not then have been such a dazzling white, but a less distracting grey-green.*

on; cut out curiously into embroidery of flowers and shapes of arabesques, animals or birds or *feuillages*, and the small alleys or intervals filled with several coloured sands or dusts with much art'. Parterres of the sort he describes were frequently on a colossal scale. Contemporaries often complained of their flatness and the winds that swept across them. As a means of relieving the horizontal nature of the parterre, they needed a new look at an old garden feature: topiaries. These soon eschewed their old forms and were gradually trained into more architectural forms. Obelisks, pyramids, domes and globes, all of purest geometry, were needed to complement the chaste smoothness of the elegantly cut lawns.

Celia Fiennes, inveterate traveller, diarist, and eccentric speller wrote about English gardens just as the parterre and its topiaries triumphed over the old knot. At the great Elizabethan house, Tixall Hall, Derbyshire, she saw '. . . gravell walks full of flowers and greens and a box hedge cut finely with little trees, some cut round, and another hedge of strip'd holly cut even and some of lawrell cut even likewise . . . [This led to a flower garden]. . . divided into knots in whiche there were 14 Cyprus trees which were grown up very tall some of them and kept cutt close in four squares down to the bottom,

**FAR LEFT** *A beautiful garden populated by classic topiaries, notably the handsome crested birds a-top drums of yew. It was once more common to use holly or box for the base, and yew for the figure above, or sometimes two varieties of yew.*

**LEFT** *Topiaries can make delightful small-scale features in tiny spaces. Here, globes, spirals, and spheres strung along bare trunks, make an enchanting picture. Though box makes a good plant to use, fast growing* Lonicera nitida *can be grown too and swiftly make a topiary well worth looking at.*

towards the top they enclined to a point or spire'. And so things remained, until all was swept away by the end of the eighteenth century when the landscape movement promoted a more natural form of gardening.

In smaller gardens, the old idea of topiary survived for much longer. It was particularly tenacious in Holland, where, even at the height of the landscape craze of the eighteenth century, it was not unusual to find tiny four-square gardens, with paths and curlicues of gravel, borders of hollyhocks and 'greens', or rare plants, all decorated with balls, spirals, even animals of box, carefully tended in earthenware pots. The same gardens also contained obelisks of trellis to support some of the new and exciting climbers. Even the great houses along the River Vecht had gardens that still clung to the old modes of gardening.

Their owners must have cheered when they discovered, by 1820 or so, that even the most committed avant-garde garden theorists in Britain were beginning to regret the wholesale destruction of the old formal gardens and their topiaries during the landscape movement. It took only a decade or so before parterres were fashionable again, though often now filled with brilliant half-hardy plants from central America and South Africa. This was the great age of geraniums, verbenas, calceolarias, salvias and other bedding plants. In spite of the brilliant colour, parterres still needed topiary to give them vertical emphasis, and fashionable gardeners became interested in cottage gardens where topiaries in fanciful shapes were still sometimes seen.

Nowadays, the range of topiary shapes runs from ancient classics such as cones and birds to more modern objects like battleships and railway engines. However eccentric some of the shapes, they can all look delightful among roses and soapworts, asters and Japanese anemones. Topiary has become fashionable again and there are thriving markets for it in America and Europe.

**RIGHT** *At Bytham Castle, Lincolnshire, amusingly baggy topiaries, all probably planted in the late nineteenth century, are carried out in dark green yew, and its gold-leafed variety. Both make successful topiaries; but avoid the fastigiate form of yew, whose upright branches eventually fall open as the plant grows. Instead, use the basic species.*

# LABYRINTHS & MAZES

**ABOVE** *This impeccably clipped and sumptuously moated parterre is half-way to being a maze. The box hedges were probably once kept much smaller, and the areas enclosed planted with flowers. It makes a fine counterpoint to the grass plat beyond, and the forested hills in the distance.*

Mazes are often confused with the ancient labyrinth, but puzzle mazes with their branched paths and dead ends are a comparatively recent feature; the earliest puzzle mazes were planted in the Renaissance gardens of Europe. Labyrinths are much more ancient; their spiral patterns go back to the Bronze Age in Europe, and perhaps beyond. Ancient Egyptian labyrinths date from at least 1800–1700 BC, older than the oldest found in Crete, though equally ancient ones have been found in India. In many cultures labyrinths are called Troy towns. The term itself is ancient: an Etruscan vase shows the pattern and labels it as the city of Troy. The classic spiral pattern was even carved on the Troy stones used by wise women, who traced the pattern with a finger to induce a trance.

All labyrinths have unbranched pathways that lead, in however complex a manner, to the centre, and seem to have had magical and mystical significance that has lasted into recent times. Turf-cut labyrinths may mark the pattern of ancient spiral dances, like the Greek crane dance. Today, garden labyrinths can either be cut out of grass, or like some ancient labyrinths, be made out of lines of boulders.

While the development of the ancient magical labyrinths as a garden feature is a modern idea, the puzzle maze is a Renaissance one. Gardens of that period were filled with jokes and conundrums. When visitors tired of being drenched with water from hidden fountains, or watching the automata in the grotto, they could get lost in the maze. The path to the centre of a puzzle maze branched, with all but one branch

**RIGHT** *The grass-cut maze at Chenies Manor, Buckinghamshire, reproduces a scheme shown in a portrait of the manor's sixteenth-century owner, Edward, Lord Russell. Though mimicking a proper turf labyrinth, here there are false turns and dead ends, warranting the ambiguous motto 'Fate will Find a Way' found on the painting. The replica was made in 1983.*

**BELOW** *The amusing freeform puzzle at Glendurgan, near Falmouth, Devon is made of cherry laurel. There are three quarters of a mile of pathway, and the hedges take a gardener two weeks to prune. The whole job needs to be done five times a year. The scheme was designed by the owner Alfred Fox in 1833.*

having dead ends. Most had high hedges, and when people entered they were deprived of any sense of direction. The word 'amazed' perfectly describes the frustrating sensation of being lost in one.

The first puzzle mazes were recorded in 1494. By 1660 whole books of maze patterns appeared, which were also used in marquetry, embroidery, and perhaps confectionery as well. A fine example is *Hortorum Viridariorumque Formae* by Jan Vredeman de Vries, published in Antwerp in 1583. Its mazes have only low hedges. William Lawson, writing in 1618, says, in his delightful *A New Orchard and Garden*, that he prefers 'Mazes well framed to a Man's height, which may perhaps make your Friend wander in gathering Berries till he cannot recover himself without your help'. His mazes may have been planted up with wild strawberries.

The largest maze ever was made in 1607 at Mantua. The paths were wide enough for horses and carriages; just as well, for the shortest route to the centre was two miles. The oldest surviving puzzle maze in Britain is at Hampton Court, and dates from 1690. Even during the landscape movement, they were popular items at tea and pleasure gardens, and at big country houses. There is still considerable interest in mazes and labyrinths and many puzzle mazes are being planted in large gardens, while the smallest cottage garden can have a simple labyrinth of stones or cut turf beneath an apple tree.

## in its setting: topiary
## HASELEY COURT, ENGLAND

The enchanting topiary garden at Haseley Court, Oxfordshire, survived by lucky chance. Part of a grand Victorian garden, it was planted during the revival of topiary that took place in the 1890s. However, the garden and the house went through harsh times, especially during and after the Second World War. While the rest of the garden and the house gradually became derelict, the topiaries were adopted by a local man, Mr Shepherd, who kept them trimmed. In the 1950s, an intrepid and energetic American, Mrs Nancy Lancaster, fell in love with Haseley Court and bought and restored it. The walled garden was sumptuously replanted and the razed medieval foundations became gardens.

The topiary survived and flourished. The yew and box topiaries are set in a sunken rectangle that was probably once a bowling or croquet lawn. The outer boundary of alternating tall yew cylinders and clipped standards of Portugal laurel *Prunus lusitanica* makes a combination of shapes that has been popular since at least the seventeenth century. The pieces were probably always intended to look like chessmen, though the form of topiaries can easily change from decade to decade. When one of the 'pawns' died in 1973, a neighbouring piece was allowed to grow into a 'knight' to fill up the space.

Mrs Lancaster surrounded the topiaries with soft-coloured lavenders and silver-leafed santolinas. She put more topiary into the rest of the garden. Clipped bays grow in grey and white Versailles tubs, and spirally clipped cones of yew emerge from ivy-clad bases on the medieval foundations.

*1 The chess set topiary garden contains 32 pieces. Although they are often called chessmen, only eight are easily recognizable as chess pieces. The larger topiaries, like the tall columns, are cut from yew, the smaller pieces from box.*

*2 Exuberant drifts of lavender make an exciting contrast with the dark green of the box and yew. The vigorous flower stalks work splendidly with the formal topiary shapes, which can also look good with romantic plantings of grey-pink oriental poppies, dark blue irises and lupins.*

# CENTREPIECES

# CENTREPIECES THAT MAKE AN IMPACT

A centrepiece can be a very powerful design element in the garden. Even the simplest of objects in the tiniest of spaces can make an immensely exciting impact. Centrepieces are features and do not have to be centrally placed in the space, though many are. However, good ones are absolutely central to a garden's design, and hold their part of the garden together.

Centrepieces can be as simple as a pot of geraniums, or as grand as a piece of sculpture. They can just as well be fun and fake, as made of bronze and marble. Centrepieces can have huge variety from a glorious garden pavilion to a painted board cut-out that looks like a piece of theatre set. They can be antiques, but in modern gardens they range from stainless steel obelisks that reflect four glittering slices of garden, to a beautiful piece of natural stone. Every garden culture, from ancient China to eighteenth-century America, has used centrepieces to set off the design of their gardens.

All centrepieces create a focus for both gardener and garden, which pulls the design together. They lead the eye into the garden and extend an invitation to explore. They can also make the termination of a view, keeping the eye within the garden. This can be especially useful in small spaces, where the real view may be of other houses or uninteresting city scenes.

Some centrepieces are centred at the end of the garden vista. Others stand where garden paths cross, indeed that special part of a garden is strong, and has often been emphasized by a sundial, or a big planter, sometimes even a pool, a rose arch or a pavilion. As centrepieces give the garden style in winter as well as in summer, choose them after careful consideration.

OVERLEAF *A piece of simple woodland planting, with ferns and hostas as ground cover, is given instant excitement by using a centrepiece, here a dramatic sculpture of a winged boy with bow and arrow. The statue might not work in a domestic or gallery setting, but looks perfect here.*

RIGHT *This energetic 'Fu Dog', or 'Lion of Buddha', may have begun life as a temple guardian. Now he looks after a garden. Animals of his sort usually come in pairs, the male resting his paw on a ball of ribbons (this one has an enamelled solid ball), while his mate rests hers on a pup. They ward off evil spirits, and are much used in Chinese geomancy. This one makes a perfect point beneath an autumnal maple.*

We have always used the path of the sun through the heavens to mark the time of day. In the gardens of the Roman Empire it was common to find columns cut to mark the place of the midday shadow falling on their shafts. However, sundials were also widely used. They were often a block of stone, with a concave face on the south side, and an iron gnomon (arm) at the top to cast the shadow. Twelve grooves radiating from the gnomon told the time of day.

Rather similar sundials were found on the walls of houses or mounted on gable ends in medieval Europe. They were also placed in more public places, and church porches or the village cross sometimes had one so that the local inhabitants could use them. Sundials were once objects of value and veneration (wizards and warlocks needed sundials that told the season as well as the time), and many were carved and gilded. They

became garden ornaments only when reliable watches became widespread in the eighteenth century.

Sundials are one of the great garden classics, especially when they stand in a drift of lavenders, catmints and soft pinky-mauve roses. John Claudius Loudon, an immensely influential and prolific garden writer of the early nineteenth century wrote that sundials were '. . . venerable and pleasing decorations and should be placed in conspicuous frequented parts, as in the intersection of principal walks (where) . . . the note they give of time may be readily recognised by the passenger.' Many were in use as garden features in the 1820s.

These practical and decorative timepieces tell the time in various ways, most usually by the shadow of a gnomon. The gnomon is a spike or wire orientated north-

# SUNDIALS & ARMILLARY SPHERES

*ABOVE The gnomon of this fine contemporary sundial, set in plantings of close-clipped thyme, is a thin metal rod, nattily supported by a curved section of iron. Easily built, it would make a perfect centrepiece for a sunny patio or yard.*

south to cast the least shadow at midday, and which moves across a flat plate engraved with the hours. Sundials can also be engraved with mottos, some of which, like the well-known *Sic transit gloria mundi*, (the glories of this world pass) or the equally gloom-laden 'We all must . . . [die]' can cast a slight chill over the sunniest day.

As decorative features for the garden, or for a wall or gable of the house, sundials have been popular since the sixteenth century, though in those days they had a real function as well. The great vogue for sundials as decorative objects followed on from Loudon's words and reached its height in the late nineteenth and early twentieth centuries. Such was the demand for good plates that old ones were reproduced in great numbers. Treat any dates that they bear with suspicion. One very popular plate called the Chepstow Dial was reproduced by Whites Pyghtle Works in 1910. The original early eighteenth-century plate was found in a garden in Chepstow, in Wales.

Though most sundial plates stand on similar balusters, other supports have also been used. In the early eighteenth century, Indian and blackamoor sculptures were often

pressed into service as supports for sundials. Sometimes stone pillars dramatically supported a whole range of dials, telling the time in London or Antwerp, and places as far afield as Moscow and New Amsterdam.

Victorian gardeners liked sundials made only with flowers. They used plants such as the four-o-clock flowers (*Mirabilis jalapa*), whose translucent cerise and scarlet flowers open only at tea time. They have a wonderful perfume all night, and close the following morning. It is a perfect plant to have around any dial or seat.

Today, armillary spheres have also become garden features. In ancient Greece, astronomers used them as teaching tools. They take their name from the metal circles (*armillae* in Latin), that demonstrate the structure of the universe, together with the positions and the orbits of the various heavenly bodies. Huge numbers were made with the reawakening of astronomy in the sixteenth century but, gilded and engraved, they were too valuable for the garden. They became garden centrepieces during the nineteenth century, and are still popular in both European and American gardens.

Sundials and armillary spheres are still much in demand, whether antique or contemporary. Though clumsy examples are easily available, it is worth hunting for those made by the many talented craftsmen and women of today who find them exciting. A number of sundial societies exist for serious enthusiasts.

Statues have always fascinated gardeners. Early statuary was sacred, and devoted to images of the gods, or humans of god-like beauty. By the beginning of the last millennium, the sculptors of the Roman Empire made garden statuary of heroes and emperors, as well as figures of mythology. When classical statues were discovered in the

# STATUARY TO CATCH THE EYE

BELOW *This marvellous eye-catcher, an indolent woman seated graciously in a shell, gazes outward towards the lake at Lomonosov, a park near St Petersburg. Curiously, her mood affects the whole scene, and shows how powerfully a statue can influence its surroundings.*

ruins of ancient Rome and its environs during the Renaissance, they were all, sacred or profane, taken and used to decorate the gardens of the wealthy. Such was the demand for Roman artefacts, that the statues became items of trade, and aristocrats all over Europe collected them. As demand quickly outstripped supply, copyists moved in and began to create a celestial collection of gods and goddesses

However, gardeners who wanted a statue as a centrepiece to their garden realized that Hercules and Diana were out of place in small or urban spaces. A range of statuary with less pretension was developed and assorted nymphs and fauns, Greek philosophers, shepherd, shepherdesses and putti became the staple produce of garden

sculptors. The range was exciting, for it meant that garden owners could give a coherent theme to their gardens, without having to live up to the presence of the gods.

While the great classic sculptures were usually made of marble, the new garden statuary used the lesser materials of cast lead, ordinary stone, or ceramics. Today, that

range has expanded to include concrete in various forms, glass fibre, plastics, stainless steel, and even corrugated iron. Extraordinarily, whatever the material used, the presence of an image of an animal or a human, let alone a god in the garden can have a very special quality about it, which stimulates both imagination and association.

Some of the most charming garden statuary ever made was created by the prolific John Cheere (1709–1787). Perhaps he took up the trade of garden ornament maker because he had less talent than his brother, Sir Henry Cheere, a famous sculptor knighted for his work. John Cheere's workshops created lead-work images of peasants making hay and merry, selling fruit, or playing Pan pipes. These decorous figures were immensely popular throughout the eighteenth century, even in gardens where classical gods and

**ABOVE** *Imagination, not expense, is what makes a perfect centrepiece. In this Dutch garden, a piece of painted board becomes an eighteenth-century gentleman among his flowers. Like some of the painted figures once employed to inhabit empty rooms, this charming example has an impact vastly greater than its cost, and it makes the onlooker laugh.*

**RIGHT** *This nonchalant bumpkin on his pedestal is still painted in his original colours. Probably from the workshops of John Cheere, or perhaps one of his copyists, the statue makes a perfect foil to the yew hedge. In a tiny garden, he would look good against an ivy-covered wall, flanked by seats and big pots of heliotrope or acid-yellow hibiscus.*

goddesses were also admired. It is not now clear whether the lead-work peasants were meant to represent actual workers on garden and estate; Cheere's more frivolous figures may, in fact, have represented aristocrats playing at *fêtes champêtres*, a world away from real milkmaids and gamekeepers. However, some details of the costumes that these figures wear were once gilded, and no peasant would have sported such extravagances.

Individual castings of John Cheere's figures differ from one another in details such as buttons, pockets and so on, as these were often made anew for each casting. Cast

**RIGHT** *Terms like these were used in ancient Roman estates and gardens to mark the boundaries, facing outward to the hostile world. This one, vigorous and handsome, is an eighteenth-century example at Hartwell House, Buckinghamshire. He was probably never a guardian, but one of a series designed to stand against a wall or hedge. A single term of this quality would make the perfect closure to a garden path, but would have to face inward; not classically correct, but visually stunning.*

in hollow sections, each figure was assembled around a strong iron armature to keep it from sagging, and the ironwork was anchored into the pedestal that supports the whole figure. They were once painted in life-like colours, and cost around £20 a pair.

Another classic piece of statuary popular in seventeenth- and eighteenth-century gardens was the term. Confusingly, terms are sometimes called herms. Either word is perfectly correct, but whichever is used, the figure is a head and shoulder bust of a godling or philosopher, mounted on a tapering pedestal. Late Roman terms were frequently portraits of other mythological and historic figures. Wealthy Romans often displayed terms of important Greek rulers and philosophers in their houses and gardens to suggest their own intelligence and educational background.

Architecturally speaking, terms are caryatids, but in gardens they are used as freestanding ornaments, not as supports for a roof beam. Terms are named after Terminus, the minor god who was sacred to estate boundaries. Terminus's other duties were to prevent disputes between neighbours, and guard against interlopers, so he was always placed to look outward, facing boundaries and exits to the garden. Without feet, he was anchored to the spot on permanent duty. Many copies of ancient Roman originals were made in eighteenth-century Rome. Most were made by second-grade sculptors, unless they were for very grand estates. In England, the renowned sculptor Rysbrack might be asked to do them. Those he made for Lord Burlington cost £8 each.

Rysbrack made garden sculpture for many aristocratic gardeners, and his work survives in quantity at gardens like Stowe, Buckinghamshire, where, for Lord Cobham, he shared the commission for carving busts of ancient British worthies with Peter Scheemaker, another prominent sculptor. These busts were made to decorate the niches of the curving stone structure designed by William Kent, the first of the great English landscape gardeners, and meant to demonstrate how the moral fibre of the nation was in alarming decline.

In addition to human worthies and gods, the gardens of ancient Rome also had statues of animals, not only the wolf-mother of Romulus and Remus, but beasts such as the dog of Alcibiades, the Athenian general and politician; the boar of Calydon from Greek mythology, and others. The idea was enthusiastically taken up in eighteenth-century gardens, where the animal statues could supply a touch of frozen violence and threat. Gory scenes such as lions attacking horses, or wolves attacking a female mastiff and her pups were popular subjects. Pairs of lions were more peaceful, and are still popular today. Early lions were modelled on a famous pair of large cats created for the Medici family in Renaissance Florence. They were often used at doors and especially beside flights of stairs leading up to doorways.

The eighteenth-century sculptor Peter Scheemaker supplied a number of animal sculptures for important gardens designed by William Kent. The boars, wolves and lions for Lord Burlington's garden at Chiswick House near London, were made in the 1730s and 1740s. Some of these statues were so widely admired that they were copied in lead by John Cheere, and sold to many other gardens in Britain.

ABOVE *A modern interpretation of the Roman term, this serene stoneware head is by potter Patricia Volk. It is every bit as strong as the eighteenth-century examples, and could be used in a similar way. Its smaller scale would make it perfect at a crossing of paths, or beside a still pool planted with Japanese irises and waterlilies.*

Lions were also sculpted by the Italian sculptor Canova, who did sleeping lions at the foot of a monument to Pope Clement XIII in Rome. The sculptor worked on the monument between 1783 and 1792, and when it was finished Canova's lions became models for many garden lions that were widely popular after that date. Even in America, where such pretension to grandeur was frowned upon, lions and lionesses were in great demand as garden ornaments. This was especially true after the American Civil War, when iron foundries turned away from making armaments and used their skills and equipment to make garden ornaments instead.

But other animals were popular too. In France, the most prolific and popular animal modeller was Alfred Jacquemart, of the Val d'Osne Foundry. His models, whether dogs, wolves, boars, or birds, were often marked 'AJ', and had a wide market, especially when scaled down and cast in bronze. These smaller-scale models were intended for mantelpieces, not the garden, and cost as much as five times more. In England, the Coalbrookdale Company copied the same range of animals, and employed sculptors and modellers to keep the range up-to-date with the rapidly changing aesthetic tastes of the period.

Garden statuary presents gardeners with a two-edged sword. The quality can become terribly debased, and it is easy to overload the garden with statues. In *The Villa Gardener*, published in 1850, Jane Loudon, wife of the garden writer John Claudius Loudon, writes of a famous London garden of the day 'We are aware that there are many persons, of a simple and severe taste, who will think that the Lawrencian Villa is too highly ornamented with statues and sculptures; but allowance must be made for individual taste, for devotion to the subject, and for the limited extent of the place. Were Mrs Lawrence in possession of a villa of one hundred acres, there can be no doubt that she would display on her lawn a taste as appropriate to a residence of that extent, as the taste she has displayed at Drayton Green.'

Mrs Lawrence, the owner of the highly ornamented garden, may not have noticed the barbs. Indeed, she rather set the tone of gardening for the rest of the century. All over Europe, huge numbers of terracotta manufacturers, marble sculptors and masons produced a staggering array of garden statuary. Much of it pretended to be Roman or Greek, but in the search for the 'tasteful', classical energy and excitement got lost. Simpering Venuses, variously draped, abound, as do insipid images of Dionysus and Hercules. Sentiment and mawkishness won over all other qualities, culminating, in the late nineteenth century, in the creation of the garden gnome.

Though many of today's garden sculptures imitate antiques, an entirely modern piece can look superb. It does not have to be a Henry Moore or an Elizabeth Frink. Modest sculptures can work just as well. These new pieces are often made in interesting materials such as stainless steel or glass fibre, as well as natural stone. They may be figures or animals, but abstract sculptures can look stunning in both formal and wild gardens. As with so much of gardening, imagination is all.

**ABOVE** *Twice the size of a domestic cat, this ceramic lion looks as if he is waiting for the next saucer of milk. Some garden lions are much larger and much more ferocious, and eye visitors ascending steps, or entering the garden, as if their next meal. Vicious or dozy, they are all part of a garden tradition that dates at least from the Renaissance.*

LEFT *A stunning modern take on the old idea of making animal sculptures a focal point in the garden, these enchanting corrugated iron elephants, almost a herd, are by Jeff Thomson. Witty, and filled with life and movement, their rusty, battered surfaces make them quite at one with the exuberant garden.*

RIGHT *Old Place Farm, Kent, has sheep in its garden, though these are not grazing the flowers, but immobile and made from chicken wire. Sheep sculptures have been used as visual jokes in gardens for at least a hundred years. These are particularly pretty, though the run-off from the galvanized wire might poison near-by plants, so do not let the sheep graze near rarities.*

A grand container, if suitably large and not liable to be overwhelmed by its plants, makes an excellent centrepiece. The grandest of container centrepieces is undoubtedly a Venetian well-head. Every square and private house in Venice once had a well, and well-heads were made to protect and define the well. The marvellous city of Venice had huge numbers of them from early medieval times. However necessary and ubiquitous, many well-heads were expensively made of hard, white Istrian marble, or green and red Rosso Verona. Many were carved too, though the conservative nature of the designs were used over a long period and makes examples hard to date. A large number of well-heads have sockets for wrought-iron overthrows, which supported pullies to lift the buckets more easily and some of these are still found in gardens.

However, water was piped into the city around 1900, just when gardeners in northern Europe became interested in anything Venetian, following the publication of John Ruskin's book *The Stones of Venice*. Now that wells were no longer in use huge numbers of well-heads were removed from their native city and shipped northward to grace gardens. Like statuary from Rome in the previous century, demand soon outstripped supply, and many copies of well-heads were made in Italian workshops.

# WELL-HEADS, PLANTERS & URNS

Still, genuine or fake a well-head really does make a romantic feature in a garden, though it is at its most romantic if set over a proper well. Most look best mounted on plinths to give them sufficient emphasis.

On a more domestic level, old copper boilers can make perfect centrepieces to simple country gardens. The containers, once used over glowing coals to heat pig food, or boil water, weather wonderfully. The green-blue patina they develop sets off to perfection tousled masses of pinks or penstemons, or blue green grasses or *Melianthus*.

At the other end of the social scale, elegant urns were used as classic centrepieces. Indeed, even aristocratic gardeners turned their hand to designing stone decorations. Some of the stone urns once at Chiswick House, near London, and attributed to the eighteenth-century garden designer William Kent, were actually designed by his patron Lord Burlington.

The most expensive material much used in England was Portland stone, but eighteenth-century garden urns were often made of Bath stone, which was less expensive and still an attractive colour. However, it was coarse grained and soon became covered in moss. A fact that suits romantic-minded modern gardeners, who cannot get their ornaments mossy quickly enough, and soak new ones with milk, soot, soil, and other secret recipes to grow green velvet. Bath stone did not suit the eighteenth-century architect Nicholas Hawksmoor, who refused to use it in London, even though it made wonderful buildings in Bath.

In Italy, where marble is so abundant, it is still used to create a vast range of garden urns. Gardeners can make excellent central focal points from these marble urns. These centrepieces are so strong visually, that they work every bit as well in formal parterres as they do in shaggy and informal gardens.

*RIGHT A perfect centrepiece for a country garden is made by an old copper boiler, set upon paved paths, with generous plantings of old-fashioned flowers such as marigolds and catmint. It is far more effective than merely having a central planting bed, and makes an excellent container for an invasive grass, or some of the more rampant mints.*

**LEFT** *This handsome urn is a modern copy of one designed by William Kent for the poet Alexander Pope's fanciful garden at Twickenham, near London. There, the original was set among bosky groves and grassland. Here, its copy looks equally compelling among the formally clipped box of a parterre.*

**BELOW** *Although the prim planting does not allow climbers to make use of it, this Venetian well-head still sports its iron superstructure. Well-heads were copied in huge numbers in the early 1900s. This one, at Brook Cottage, near Banbury in Oxfordshire, follows early medieval examples, and is splendidly displayed on a plinth at the top of steps, giving it extremely high visual impact.*

Of all the centrepieces that a garden can have, the most desirable and useful is a garden retreat. Most gardeners want a garden house, whether it is just a simple shed on an allotment, or a marble pavilion perched on the edge of a misty lake. Perhaps it is a reflection of the earliest Mesopotamian gardens, where the divisions between gardens and living quarters were more fluid than in modern times.

Garden retreats have been built by a wide range of people from tzars to factory workers. The building materials are just as varied: grandly of bronze, gold, stone and marble, and modestly of trelliswork, rustic timber, corrugated iron, and old doors. There is, today, a thriving trade in North America and Europe for prefabricated summerhouses and gazebos, as well as sheds, teepees, and meditation huts. However grand or modest, a seat in a garden retreat allows the same feelings of genial relaxation or contented contemplation, whether it is made of dressed stone, or bent branches and tarpaulin.

Though ancient Roman gardens had arbours and damp grottos, there seem to have been few garden houses in medieval Europe. Those that were built were distant

# THE PLEASURE OF GARDEN RETREATS

echoes of the East; not all Crusaders were arrogant barbarians, and a surprising number found the beauty of the Saracen gardens they sacked a revelation. Some of the Crusaders carved themselves estates from the lands they visited, particularly on islands like Sicily and Malta, and built themselves gardens filled with pavilions in the Saracen style. Even those Crusaders who returned home built themselves fine gardens and pavilions that were influenced by the Middle East.

It was really the Renaissance which was, as with so much else in the garden, the great age of the garden pavilion in northern Europe and enormous numbers of delightful buildings were erected during the period. The stone pavilions have survived, often at the ends of terraces, or centred on some axis of a garden. But many were built from timber, and sometimes, even trellis and have long since disappeared.

The inverately nosy visitor and diarist Celia Fiennes visited many garden pavilions in the early eighteenth century. Her diaries show how summerhouses were used as centrepieces in the design of the garden, as well as in the lives of the owners. While at Mount Edgecumbe near Plymouth in Devon, she wrote:'. . . there is a long walke from one part of the front down to the waterside [where] there is a fine terrace walled in . . . with open gates in the middle, and a summer house at either end . . . it [is] esteemed by me the finest seat I have seen'.

However, summerhouses were not only for the rich and aristocratic. Many European cities, particularly in the Netherlands, were ringed by areas of tiny out-of-town gardens, each with a simple and undemonstrative garden pavilion. The tradition is old,

*LEFT This lovely garden pavilion makes a wonderful place to sit on a hot summer afternoon, and is even better on a late summer evening. The building itself makes a strong statement in the garden, offering a counterpoint to the burgeoning flowers. Buildings like this are as enjoyable close to the house as they are at the end of a long walk.*

RIGHT *A number of seventeenth-century canal houses in Amsterdam still have one of these trellis pavilions, shady retreats with room for a few chairs and a table, as a centrepiece at the end of their narrow gardens. Though fun to use, their main function is to make a dramatic feature when seen from the private rooms of the main house.*

LEFT *Wirework was a popular material for garden ornaments around the middle of the nineteenth century. Frequently used for plant stands, chairs and tables, wirework was also used for whole pavilions, often called rosaries after the plants that were meant to scramble over them. This one was designed for a crossing of paths, and bird cages would have hung in its dome.*

ABOVE *A modern version of a trellis pavilion has been constructed with minimum expense, but given vast style, privacy, and mosquito-free evenings, by an inner awning of net. Simple to make, fun to use, it still offers a clever way of focusing the garden view.*

dating back to at least the mid-sixteenth century. The artist Laurens Vincentz van der Vinne (1658–1729), shows a charming picture of Dutch garden houses in his *View of the River Spaarne from the Landing Stage in front of Spaarnhout*, drawn in 1682. It shows the riverbank thickly built up with summer houses of different designs, several on two stories, many with balconies for views over the water with its boats and fishermen. The houses are very close-set, which could be a problem: in the nearby city of Haarlem, summerhouses were forbidden because of the intense overcrowding of buildings and consequent fire risks. However, gardeners were allowed to have tool sheds and rain shelters. Summerhouses in the city were banned as early as 1593, so areas south of the city developed as small plots whose owners could have as grand or as simple summerhouses as their hearts desired.

Delightful summerhouses like these continued in their development right through the seventeenth century. However, Dutch aristocrats had them too; Huis ten Bosch, the modest palace of William of Orange, later king of England, had a terrace with a matched pair of grand but conventional pavilions, designed in 1645. They were swathed in vines and other climbers.

North America has largely followed English and Dutch traditions. Indeed, America's love affair with the summerhouse started in the seventeenth century and continued into the eighteenth century. In 1705, Robert Beverly of Virginia was enchanted when hummingbirds fanned his face with their wings near a 'Summer House set round with the Indian Honey-suckle'. In 1794, Samuel McIntire built an elegant two-storey teahouse in Elias Hasket Derby's garden in Salem, Massachusetts. Thomas Jefferson provided a number of lovely garden pavilions at Monticello, his garden in Virginia, and there are pretty ones to be seen in Williamsburg.

Until the twentieth century, American writers regarded Europe as their inspiration. Andrew Jackson Downing, the first all-American garden writer, who wrote during the 1840s, followed European garden developments carefully, and like many of his sources, encouraged his readers to have covered seats, moss houses, and rustic pavilions, though constantly bearing in mind the American distaste for aristocratic show. In 1870, Frank J. Scott suggested creating a living summerhouse by roping together the tops of six hemlocks planted in a hexagon, following the ancient idea from Arab Spain, where junipers were bound with roses and jasmine to make dining pavilions.

A more recent American author, Mary Northend, wrote *Garden Ornaments* in 1916. She was obviously a fan of garden retreats: 'One should, if possible, when planning the garden, include a summer house. There is no more enjoyable feature that can be constructed in the grounds.' How right she was.

*LEFT Set in a Californian garden this modern pavilion is used for the increasingly popular practice of meditation. Its steeply pitched roof and powerful supports give it movement and life among the trees. It offers fine views of the garden, and helps to create its mood.*

*RIGHT Chinese and Japanese gardens have included garden pavilions for at least 3,000 years. All are marvellously sited and designed. Once European gardeners discovered them, they had a strong influence. Many eighteenth- and nineteenth-century European gardens have one or more chinoiserie buildings, as much for their impact on the garden design, as for contemplation, or the making of tea. This fine example, is at Cliveden, in Buckinghamshire.*

A garden lit at night has, for centuries, been a magical experience. The emperors of ancient China delighted in nocturnal boating parties, and the pleasure of seeing their gardens at night. They filled the lakes of their palace gardens with boats bearing hundreds of paper lanterns. Louis XIV turned his vast gardens at Versailles into a mysterious and smoky paradise for great occasions known as *illuminations*. The walks, bosquets (light woodland) and leafy green pavilions were lit by thousands of flaring torches. Mogul princes and Indian maharajas created gardens in which water tumbled

# LIGHTING AS A FOCAL POINT

over marble walls carved with niches for oil lamps. These niched walls, known as *chimikana*, were either to one side of a tank of still water, or formed four-sided basins. Each niche held a tiny bowl, sometimes of coloured glass, with oil and a wick. In less elaborate water gardens, rafts bearing candles were floated on the dark surface, and the women of the harem could enjoy the night perfume of tuberose and double *Brugmansia*.

From the sixteenth century, Japanese gardeners developed dozens of forms of stone lantern. These lanterns, marvellous objects in themselves, were made to light the

**LEFT** *At Port Lympne, Kent, uplighters buried in the soil throw these terms into dramatic light and shade. Pure drama, of course, especially as they stand against black 'flats' of yew hedging, but they give these statues plenty of life after dark. The curl of drapery on the column is a tactful allusion to what would have been explicit on a Roman original.*

path towards the tea ceremony. Bowls of sesame seed oil and wicks provided the light, and the openings in the lanterns were covered with little screens made of bamboo and rice paper to shelter the flame.

Among the great classics are torches of all kinds, and Chinese paper, and Japanese stone lanterns, but there are many others. Glass storm lanterns, Moorish or Indian tin and glass lanterns, and old stable lanterns with paraffin burners, all qualify and look marvellous in the garden at night. Placed on retaining walls, or by steps, or alongside the lily pool, or, if suitable, hung in the branches of a tree, lanterns can make beautiful centrepieces in, and bring real enchantment to, the night garden.

Electric lighting in the garden can be fun, but is trickier to handle. Though it is flexible, there is always the temptation to over light, using levels more appropriate to indoors. Over-lit gardens can look bleak and unmagical. However, uplighters below a handsome tree can make magic, as they also add drama to features like sculptures or trellis work obelisks. As in Mogul gardens, light and water can create a powerful mood, especially if using tiny low-voltage lamps that have hardly more light than stars.

Ecologically minded gardeners will be interested in self-charging lights, which use small solar panels on the top surface of the lamp. In sunny gardens, they are useful, and have a quality of light much closer in strength and colour to candlelight. Some of these contemporary lights have sufficient quality to become classics.

**BELOW** *Garden lighting designers usually try to hide the actual light source, but here is an interesting reversal of that idea. The harshness of a brilliant fibreoptic source is broken up by a hammered and coiled piece of lead sheet. Designed by Mike Cedar, this is a modern interpretation of the flambeaux once used to light Versailles.*

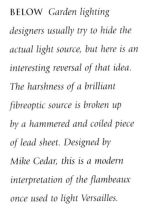

**BELOW** *Almost any sort of lantern works well in the garden, but this stone lantern in the gardens of the Shimak House, in the Geisha Quarter of Kanazawa, Japan, must be the ultimate classic. It gives a night-time picture of immense beauty, and makes a covetable garden feature.*

**1** The main centrepiece of the garden at Villa Garzoni is this boldly carved statue of Fame. The English traveller William Beckford saw it when he visited the villa in 1780. Fame's trumpet was once supplied by a local stream. Now it is motor driven, as is the water staircase below her.

**2** A laurel-wreathed statue, one of many that make exciting views all along the terraces, looks out over the lower garden, and the circular pools designed by Diodati. The garden is lined with winding arbours, and is filled with parterres, topiary and a small zoo.

## in its setting: centrepieces
### VILLA GARZONI, ITALY

Perched high on a rock, the Villa Garzoni was originally a medieval castle. It was bought by the Garzoni family in 1652, who began to convert the ancient stronghold into a great villa. The garden was separated from the castle by a deep ravine, so a bridge was built to link the two. The bones of the garden were already in place, with Renaissance terraces and linking stairways. It rapidly became one of the most spectacular of Italian baroque gardens. The great central axis was turned into a water staircase. The new centrepiece was a stone figure of Fame, whose spouting trumpet and rivulets still cascade down to feed an enchanting walled pool. The severe formality of Renaissance design was much softened, and the formal elements allowed to merge into the surrounding forests and vineyards.

The garden was revamped in 1786 by the local architect Ottavio Diodati who had rather backward-looking taste and loved elaborate decoration. He added many terracotta pots and figures to the balustrades, a green theatre and a bathing pavilion. Diodati also created numerous water jokes that operated from the villa, so the owner could soak friends exploring the garden.

Although overloaded with incident, the garden shows how to use statuary of all sizes as centrepieces, and how to create interesting views by using clusters of objects. Above all, it demonstrates how magical can be the contrast between greenery and feature. Garzoni is a garden composed of centrepieces; a wonderful place, playful, and marvellously detailed.

**3** Sunning himself so elegantly in a curved bracket between a baroque column and a balustrade, this figure of Pan is only part of Garzoni's overall scheme. However, he and his support would make a major centrepiece in a smaller and more serene garden.

**4** The extraordinary central axis of the garden at Villa Garzoni was first set out in the sixteenth century, but altered in the 1650s and the 1780s. The result is formal, yet luscious, and shows what an exuberant combination can be made by using luxuriant vegetation and inanimate but handsome features.

# SEATING

# RECLINING IN WELL-DESIGNED COMFORT

Fair weather, or foul weather, to have at least one seat in the garden is absolutely essential. Good, comfortable seating enables you to enjoy your garden and most garden cultures have produced classics. Gardeners of the Roman Empire often used chairs from the house, but contemporary accounts tell of the rush to get them indoors during a sudden storm. Pliny the Younger talks of marble garden seats, and many benches have been excavated. Roman gardens also had *triclinia*, platforms of brick, masonry or turf, where diners reclined.

Seating areas were fundamental to the gardens of the ancient Middle East, though the actual seating was of cushions and carpets based on nomadic traditions. In China, stools of lacquered wood or earthenware barrels have been used for at least 600 years. Elegant wooden chairs, used by the honoured elderly, were often made in expensive materials, and were sometimes used in garden pavilions. In Europe, turf seats followed on from Roman originals, and were extensively used well into the Renaissance. By then, stone was popularly used to recreate Roman antique seating. Roman influence continued when eighteenth-century landscape designers like William Shenstone had their carefully sited garden seats engraved with lines from Virgil and Horace.

The great age of the garden seat was the nineteenth century, when the Industrial Revolution created the wealth for more people to have gardens and features to put in them. In addition to wood and stone, garden seats were made in ceramics, metals and concrete. Shapes, sizes and designs were numerous, some, such as the nineteenth-century 'Osmunda' fern seat in cast iron, have never been bettered. Today, new materials, such as plastic, fibreglass and stainless steel, make garden seating more widely available and attract some great designers to create new classic designs for modern gardeners.

OVERLEAF  *Handsome Adirondack chairs are painted a splendid blue at Chanticleer, USA, although most chairs of this type are left in natural wood. Adirondack seats originated in a country garden in upstate New York in the late nineteenth century. There are now many variants, all comfortable, with good broad arms and seats.*

RIGHT  *This handsome cast-iron seat is a rare casting from the Carron Foundry, in Scotland. Its design was placed with the Public Record Office on 16 March 1846. The company was set up in 1759 to cast canon, stoves and gates, but made garden accessories after the Napoleonic Wars ceased in 1815.*

The grandest of all garden seats are made of stone or marble. Always expensive and often elaborately carved, such seats give grandeur to big gardens as well as small ones. In stone, they soon accumulate lichen and moss, symbols of venerable age, and their surfaces dry fairly swiftly after rain. On a sunny summer day, even chilly marble ones are warm enough to sit on by the time the gardener needs a coffee break. However, in northern gardens, for three seasons of the year they are for show only. Cushions are essential, but can make the simplest stone seat look sumptuous, and in any case, follow long-held

# CLASSIC SEATS IN STONE & CERAMIC

**LEFT** *A copy of the Roman schola, this handsome stone bench makes a strong feature at Owl House, near Lakenhurst, Sussex and shows how fine lichened stone can look when set among flowers, here rhododendrons 'Pink Pearl' and 'Dairy Maid'.*

tradition. In the ancient gardens of the Middle East, the whole design of the garden was centred on seating areas, raised platforms that were shaded from the heat beneath pavilions, or straddled across water courses, or even in the middle of water tanks. These platforms, which were often of cool marble, were made more comfortable by spreading them with an array of cushions and carpets.

Gardeners in the Roman Empire liked stone seats too, and many benches have been excavated. The semi-circular ones that have sphinx or griffin ends are called *schola* benches, possibly because teachers could attract plenty of eye contact from pupils. The senators sat on stone seats in the Forum at Rome, and the eighteenth-century stone seats once at Chiswick House in London were modelled on them. They look brutally uncomfortable. Perhaps that was why Romans preferred *triclinia* for summer lounging and dining. These gently sloping platforms were big enough for three people. They were placed on three sides of a table, often beneath a shady pergola. The fourth side was left open so that slaves could serve the meal. Some *triclinia* were set around a raised pool instead of a table, so food could be floated from guest to guest. The platforms were

**FAR RIGHT** *A griffin chair of the type made popular by Thomas Hope from the 1820s; this terracotta version stands among the lemon trees of the Villa Garzoni, near Lucca, Italy. The design was popular throughout the rest of the nineteenth century.*

sometimes of rough timber, but most surviving ones are of stone or brick. Some were covered in decorative mosaic with matching tables. *Triclinia* are usually late Roman; early Romans ate seated at table until the earlier, Greek idea of reclining to sup became fashionable. Those with *triclinia* thought that only boors sat on seats.

In Renaissance Europe, stone seating mostly copied Roman antiques, though it was often designed into the architecture, so that benches formed part of the facade of urban palaces and public buildings, or of walls in pavilions and grottos. In grottos, the tradition continued, and in seventeenth-century Europe there are many examples, such as Rosendael, in the Netherlands. However, with the increasing scale of gardening, and the delight in larger knots and parterres, garden visitors needed somewhere to rest, or to view the design. Simple stone benches are common in great schemes like those at the

**ABOVE** *Seats are good in shade too. The back of this one, in the shelter of the grotto at Rosendael in the Netherlands, is decorated with the splendid seventeenth-century shellwork that made the garden famous. The slate seat has withstood the constant spray from the nearby joke fountains, designed to dampen tired and unwary visitors.*

château of Vaux-le-Vicomte at Seine-et-Marne, or Versailles, though illustrations of the time show that garden visitors quite happily sat on steps, balustrades, turf seats, or the rims of fountains and pools. Today's designers are making marvellous contemporary versions of simple stone benches.

Towards the end of the seventeenth century, and throughout the eighteenth and nineteenth centuries, large curved benches and seats became popular features at the end of walks, or at either end of a garden's main terraces. All are based on a Roman *schola*. End arms are often lions or griffins, though a handsome eighteenth-century example in the gardens at Stourhead has Chinese cloud-scroll designs instead. In eighteenth-century North America, stone seating is much less common, though there are simple stone benches in gardens such as those at Middleton Place gardens, Charleston, where they stand at the top of a grassy slope facing out over mirrors of water, with the Ashley river flowing slowly beyond.

While some nineteenth-century designers tried to develop their own styles, most seating harked back to the Roman Empire or ancient Greece. One of the most influential neo-classical designers was Thomas Hope, a wealthy dilettante. Fascinated by the Greek Revival, an architectural style of the late 1820s, he developed a number of classical themes enthusiastically taken up by furniture makers and interior decorators, but also by makers of garden seats. Hope's designs often had sphinxes or griffins as supports, their wings providing the back, and the seat formed from a central block decorated with anthemions and scrolls of honeysuckle. The design was widely taken up, and there are marble as well as terracotta examples. Some are as late as 1870.

In Britain, the Doulton factory cast some very colourful winged sphinxes that had sockets along their sides to take wooden planks to make the seat and back. Other ceramic griffins, known as the Pistoia design, were sold by White's, a garden decoration company. They were imported from Italy, and were equally odd, with a rather unpleasant combination of wooden slats and very glossily glazed terracotta. Other strange ceramic seats were in the rustic style, which imitated tree trunks and branches. Widely produced in Scotland, where the rustic style took strongest hold, they were made from the 1870s onward. Famous examples come from the Moss End Pottery, Glasgow, while others, that looked as if made from sage-green toffee, came from J and R Howie, of Kilmarnock.

Ceramics like terracotta were never widely used in European gardens. However, in China, barrel-shaped stools made of glazed earthenware have been popular since at least the fifteenth century, both in the open garden, but also in pavilions and garden tents. They are often associated with ceramic tables. The sixteenth-century Chinese painting, *Gathering in the Western Garden*, shows worthies of the Sung period seated on such stools. Chinese gardens had wooden stools too, taken indoors at night, whereas ceramic ones were left outside all year.

**LEFT** *Glazed barrel seats like these have been in gardens in China since the fifteenth century. At the Garden of the Humble Administrator, in Suzhou, they are set around ceramic tables, but they can be used by themselves in gardens and courtyards. Similar seats are made today.*

**RIGHT** *This beautiful, understated slate bench is a modern classic and works perfectly set against clipped box and figs. It is a contemporary version of the benches that were popular in seventeenth-century gardens, which also stood among clipped box and topiaries.*

# THE ELEGANCE OF WOODEN SEATING

**LEFT** *Wheelbarrow chairs can be seen in eighteenth-century prints. They enable a single person to move an otherwise immovable piece of furniture. The architect Edwin Lutyens designed them in the twentieth century too, probably using eighteenth-century sources. The chair shown here is a modern example*

Wood is the ideal garden seat material. Easily shaped, carved and painted, it adapts easily to any style, from knobbly rustic to elegant chinoiserie, or from the grandeur of designs by William Kent to the simplicity of the park bench. Wooden seats are comfortable to sit on both in mid-winter and high summer, and can be used to bring colour and style to the garden even in the grey of winter. They can age splendidly, dry out rapidly after rain, and are warm to sit on.

Soft wood, such as pine, can be used to make garden seats. Pine is relatively inexpensive but has to be painted or treated with special preservatives to prevent rapid decay. More expensive hard woods, such as iroko, teak and cedar are much more durable. The grandest of all is oak. These more expensive woods do not need painting, last well, and age handsomely.

Classic designs are legion, varying from the traditional park bench (which always looks as if it should have an 'in memoriam' plaque on the back), to the familiar Chinese Chippendale seats, all of which date from the 1860s revival of that style. Many were produced by the firm of J P White well into the twentieth century.

Some grand seats could follow the sun. They were made with wheels at one end so that they could be pushed around the garden in pursuit of sunny spots. Among the classic movable seats are the wheelbarrow seats at Powis Castle, in Wales.

**FAR LEFT** *A handsome composite bench that would originally have been painted. From the 1850s, many iron foundries cast bench ends of various designs, some far more elaborate that this. The seats are comfortable, but by the time the wood needs replacing, the bolts that hold it in place have often rusted into immovable lumps.*

**LEFT** *A modern copy of the seat usually ascribed to architect Edwin Lutyens is an essential feature in gardens such as Sissinghurst, Kent, where its strongly architectural form works brilliantly when half-smothered in flowers. It is more comfortable if provided with cushions.*

BELOW *The eighteenth-century landscape designer William Kent created this seat for the gardens of Rousham House, Oxfordshire. Covered seats were widely used in early eighteenth-century Europe and North America, and modern copies are still made. They make comfortable and visually arresting garden features. Some had fully boarded sides for more shelter.*

Most wooden seats were fixed, like the greatest classic of all, usually attributed to the architect Edwin Lutyens, and named after him. However, he probably derived its elegant curves from eighteenth-century prints of the garden seats at Chiswick House, though these were probably copied from seventeenth-century originals, or derived from Chinese imports. In contrast, the most appealing park benches are in the Army and Navy Stores' 1913 catalogue where they are called 'man-o-war seats', largely because they were made of teak stripped from old naval ships.

Most fun, perhaps, are covered seats, described by Celia Fiennes in the early eighteenth century at Patsull House, Shrewsbury; '. . . beyond is another Garden . . . in the middle is a long. . . sheete of water, at the four corners are seates, sheltered behind and on the top and sides with boards painted, in which you sit secured from the weather and looks on the water . . .'. Covered seats were popular in America too, and advocated by the designer Andrew Jackson Downing. There are good examples at the Moffat-Ladd garden, Portsmouth, New Hampshire.

Softwood garden seats need regular painting to keep out the weather. White is conventional, brash, and can be overdone. The garden designer Gertrude Jekyll wrote: 'The common habit of painting garden seats a dead white is certainly open to criticism. The seats should be made not too conspicuous . . .'. Miss Jekyll liked them a quiet tone of green. Other colours can work well; try slate blue, especially against a dark green hedge, or peacock green amongst summer flowers, or even Chinese red with plenty of silver artemisias and purple sages. In any case, a new colour for a seat is only a pot of paint away.

*ABOVE Tree seats like this have been popular at least since medieval times. The idea is usually lovelier than the reality, for they make conversation impossible, are usually covered in twigs and bird droppings, and tree trunks are not always comfortable seat backs. However, similar seats can be found in most garden cultures.*

Seating with wooden seats and back, but with side supports of iron or steel were first made by the French firm of Barbezat et Cie. Known as *pieds de bancs*, they appeared from 1850 onwards. They could be supplied with iron seats too. Whether of iron or wood the seats were painted to look like grained pine or oak.

Wooden seats should frequently be checked for rot at peg-hole fixings, and particularly where the arms join the main framework. If the seats overwinter outdoors, stand the feet on something waterproof, or stones. Keep an eye open for buckling paintwork or rusting bolts – water may be getting into the wood beneath.

Seats made of turf were used in the ancient world, and were popular well into the Renaissance. They can be seen in medieval paintings and tapestries, where strawberries, lilies and violets flower in the roughly clipped grass. Grass seats are easily built out of a pile of unused turfs, and can last for several years without much work other than an occasional mow. The frontispiece of the late sixteenth-century book *The Gardener's Labyrinth* shows a trellis arbour with turf seats and a marble table – a lovely idea for a garden feature. Babur, Emperor of India from 1526–1530, planted his beloved plane trees on grassy platforms, so that he could lounge beneath their shade on cool verdure. In eighteenth-century France, the *Salle de Bal* in the gardens at Versailles had an amphitheatre of turf seats around the marble dance floor.

*BELOW The grass sofa is a splendid modern take on an idea that was first used in ancient Roman gardens: a turf seat is a very comfortable place to sit. Some gardeners plant meadow flowers in the turf, or use thyme or chamomile for a scented cushion, though thymes attract bees, and chamomile is more aromatic than some gardeners like. Grass seats dry surprisingly quickly after rain.*

Various metals have been used to make seats since at least Roman times. However, the great age of the metal garden seat was the nineteenth century, when hundreds of different kinds of chairs were made of cast iron. Some have become classics and are still being made. Some have never been copied, such as the 1830s' knight in armour, whose knees formed the seat, his arms the arm-rest, and his spiky visor, the head rest.

In the nineteenth century, cast-iron was always painted, though it rusts quickly if the paint cracks. Today's cast seats are often of non-rusting aluminium. There are some

# LETTING METAL TAKE THE STRAIN

**ABOVE** *The famous Gothic tracery seat first produced by Barbezat et Cie in the mid-nineteenth century makes an elegant contrast with the tall spikes of* Acanthus mollis, *one of the most architectural plants in the garden. The seat, now rusty, was probably once painted either a deep brown or olive green.*

extremely pretty cast aluminium replicas of a nineteenth-century gothic garden seat first brought out by the French firm of Barbezat et Cie in 1858. Originals, now valuable, rust quickly. The replicas will not corrode and are easier to move around the garden. The seat was copied in 1860 by Crawfords Foundry, Glasgow, and can be found in many Scottish gardens. Pretty though it is to look at, the seat is not deep enough to be comfortable for more than a ten-minute stay, although cushions help.

Many cast-iron seats were more generously built but were found to be cold to sit on, so a large number of iron founders began to cast iron sides and backs, but made the seats of timber slats. These were often painted the same colour as the ironwork. These wood and iron seats can be extremely comfortable. Popular shades in the nineteenth century were dark green, bronze, brown, and some seats were even painted red with gilded highlights.

**ABOVE LEFT** *Original wirework seats from the late nineteenth century can sometimes be found at auctions and in antique shops. In most, the seats have rusted and restoration can be difficult. Some modern wirework seats are more serviceable in the garden, but few have the grace of the originals.*

The well-known English foundry of Coalbrookdale made great classics including 'Fern and Blackberry' in six different sizes, and the firm's catalogue of 1875 lists 41 models of garden chairs and park benches. The foundry's greatest technical achievement was the now fabulously rare 'Osmunda' seat, the back of which is cast interwoven fronds of the glorious osmunda fern. Many of the cast-iron seats that now appear to be very much of the Victorian period were still being cast well into the twentieth century. Cast-iron park benches, with side supports of cast-iron and the seat of wood, can make your garden look rather like a park. However, if long enough, they can be very comfortable, though the mixture of materials usually looks awkward, except in extreme decrepitude.

Wirework seats were made from various weights of iron wire, which were twisted together in different ways. The technology became inexpensive enough to use for garden

RIGHT *Though wrought iron benches like these were superseded by cast iron, wrought iron is much lighter and more easily moved. Some benches even had castors to ease the chase for sun or shade. The slightly springy seats make them very comfortable. Although white is not an original colour, these elegant seats at the Lost Gardens of Heligan, in Cornwall, look well in luxuriant vegetation.*

furniture from around 1870, and was fashionable in conservatories, tea gardens, and urban cafés. Original pieces of wire work are now rare because they rusted. Some of the better ones are gradually being copied, and modern replicas can look exceptionally pretty in the garden. Café chairs with sprung seats made of thin strips of metal bent to shape were common from 1880 into the 1890s.

Wrought-iron seats and benches are heavier. Early examples from the 1820s are usually made from flat, reeded, strips of metal, lightly bent, and riveted together. Many were extremely elegant, though their great weakness has always been where the strips join. Good modern copies are sometimes available, and look decoratively insubstantial among summer flowers. Some folding conservatory chairs with sprung backs and seats also had wrought-iron frames. These are fun, very comfortable, and can look quite enchanting. Made around 1860, they are now, alas, hard to come by.

**LEFT** *A garden in Haarlem, in the Netherlands, shows a contemporary slant on the old 'seats-in-an-arbour' idea. These plastic chairs, in attractive colours, are 'Lord Joe' by Phillipe Starck. Their shape is related to Lloyd Loom chairs of the 1930s. The 'arbour' here is of stainless steel and polyethylene sheeting, designed by Henk Weijers.*

# STYLISH PLASTIC & TRADITIONAL TEXTILES

**LEFT** *This model of the much-loved traditional deckchair has somewhere for the gardener to prop elbows while reading the Sunday newspapers. The faded slings are set off by the greenhouse and vegetables, but would look as good on a lawn or set among much more sophisticated planting.*

ABOVE *Whatever their working history below a warship's decks or in nineteenth-century prisons, hammocks now seem symbols of lazy afternoons in the garden. This soft rope hammock, invites the gardener to a welcome snooze, as well as being a strong visual feature among the flowers.*

The earliest known use of textiles for garden seating is probably the piled cushions and rugs on which the nomadic rulers of central Asia rested once they had ceased travelling for a while and settled into their walled garden encampments. When the Romans wanted to recline, they piled cushions on *triclinia* in their shady garden courtyards. Rajahs and Caliphs did the same on the marble platforms among their fountains in Persia and India. Cushions piled up against the trunk of an old orchard tree can make a perfect place for today's garden owner to have an afternoon siesta.

One of the great classics of summer lawns is the European deckchair made of canvas and wood. In the United States, a deckchair is usually made entirely of wood but in Europe a seat of this type is known as a steamer chair. Deck chairs are great fun and come in a number of basic designs. Striped fabric is traditional for the sling, and looks better when bleached a little by the sun. Deckchairs were invented by the Merchant Navy in the late nineteenth century, and until the advent of plastics were the British garden's most popular form of seating, as they are light, cheap, and comfortable.

Plastic chairs of the white, stacking variety are ugly, but are now found in gardens worldwide. That is a shame, for the material has huge potential. Some contemporary designers, notably Phillipe Starck, have designed plastic seating that can be used in the garden. These well-designed plastic seats will become the classics of the future. However, the field is still wide open, and there is no reason why design classics cannot be made inexpensive enough to bring good design to a very wide market. For environmentally minded gardeners there are already seats and benches made of recycled plastics, though so far the movement has not created any classic pieces.

If your garden has two suitable trees, or even a wall and a tree, one of the great leisure classics is the hammock. It has an ancient history; indeed, versions are found in so many cultures that they may have evolved in prehistoric times. They were widely used by sailors from the sixteenth century onwards. Made of sail cloth, they were comfortable and space-saving beds that minimized the roll of the ship. They were slung from cleats on the ship's frame and when not in use they were rolled and stowed. Rolled, they were used as liferafts, and unrolled also as shrouds.

In North America, hammocks were considered a novelty until the 1880s, when, thanks partly to a wider version, the hammock became part of the southern 'siesta' way of life. They were often lavishly tasselled and fringed. Some of today's hammock makers supply inelegant frames on which to sling them, but the look is arid. Hammocks need foliage and dappled shade, whether their tree supports are eucalyptus and frangipani, or the old apple trees in the backyard.

# in its setting: seating
## QUINTA DOS AZULEJOS, PORTUGAL

This astonishing series of decorated seats and columns runs the entire width of the garden behind the blue-tiled house, not surprisingly called Quinta dos Azulejos (Farmhouse of the Blue Tiles). The showy walk, once much more heavily planted, leads to side walks running north and south, which are also generously provided with places to sit. All the walks are sumptuously tiled, though the actual seats are made of stone, perhaps to ensure that the seats dried swiftly after rain, or after the gardeners had watered the planting beds.

The walk along the south-facing wall of the garden, expands in its central section to make a large vine-covered arbour. Here, too, there are huge tile-backed seats, cool places from which to watch the central fountain and pool. The garden, which was created in the mid-eighteenth century was much admired by contemporaries and frequently visited by members of the Portuguese royal family, which may be why the owner Antonio Colaço Torres, continued to add to the decor. The earliest tiles he used were in traditional blue and white, while the later ones, embossed as well as painted, are from 1779, and included new colours such as orange and green.

Every vertical surface is completely tiled. Some tiles imitate marble, while others show biblical, agricultural or maritime scenes, as well as pictures of gallants and their mistresses. Many scenes are copies of engravings taken from pattern books printed in northern Europe, so the tiles are sometimes thought of as Dutch, though all of them were produced locally. Today, the *quinta* is used as a college, though the gardens at Lumiar, near Lisbon, are open every day.

1 These generous tiled seats, curved to make conversation easy, alternate with extraordinary hexagonal columns, also tiled, and topped with strange urns. The tiled seats kept visitors cool during hot Portuguese summers, and the garden once had much more shade. The ornate walk continues towards a pool and a cooling fountain.

**2** The section of garden next to the house is almost entirely devoted to seating, for seats make an edging to walks and contain the planting. The seat backs terminate in low columns that are stands for potted plants, such as tuberose, blue hyacinths, or some of the pelargoniums that reached Spain and Portugal from South Africa in the late eighteenth century.

**3** Many Portuguese gardens are decorated with tiles, some with picture panels from as early as the mid-seventeenth century. However, most of the tile pictures are single incidents on plain walls. The garden of Quinta dos Azulejos, which dates from the middle of the eighteenth century, is totally tiled, and often thought the finest of them all.

# CONTAINERS

# CLASSIC CONTAINERS FROM EARTHENWARE TO METAL

Most of the earliest functions of containers were to do with the technical aspects of gardening, especially propagation and planting. Excavations at the Hephaisteion, the great temple in the Agora of ancient Athens, revealed a row of holes in which young trees had been planted together with the earthenware pots in which they had been grown. In the gardens of the Roman Empire, pots were used for planting out lemons and vines.

Very much later, in seventeenth-century Versailles, France, Louis XIV's gardeners bought a quarter of a million flower pots a year. That vast number of pots allowed them to replant the king's gardens with new patterns of flowers as soon as one scheme was over, and another was ready for view. Even in the domestic gardens of seventeenth-century Scotland, John Reid, in his book *The Scots Gard'ner* published in 1683, suggested that 'when you find a breach by some being past the flower, you may have various annual flowers sown in pots, ready to plunge into the vacancies.'

Some plant containers were decorative, especially when the plants that grew in them were tender and had to be brought indoors for winter. Decorative pots were also used for 'rare greens', or exotic plants, so owners could show off both plant and pot. During the sixteenth century the Duke of Sermoneta displayed the rare plants he had brought from Constantinople, Paris, and Amsterdam in colourful glazed pots in his garden at Cisterna in Italy. At Woburn Abbey, Bedfordshire, in the late 1600s, grandly swagged terracotta pots were planted with orange and lemon trees, myrtles, and rare aloes from South Africa. At William of Orange's Dutch house at Zorgvliet, the Delftware pots held topiary. In China, from ancient times to the present day, beautifully proportioned pots contained bonsai, or orchids, or paeonies.

OVERLEAF *The manor house and terraced gardens of Brécy, in Normandy, France, are thought to have been designed by the great seventeenth-century designer François Mansart. The main entrance is flanked by earthenware pots filled with clipped box, and formal rows of blue painted Versailles tubs.*

RIGHT *Earthenware pots can be frivolous and elegant as well as rustic. Here, some exceptionally pretty pots, ribbed and coloured, hold topiary corkscrews of box, and flank an early nineteenth-century seat. It is a delightful arrangement; even tiny gardens need at least a pair of large scale containers to give them visual excitement.*

# CERAMIC, WOOD & STONE CONTAINERS

ABOVE *The pier that terminates a balustrade, or that flanks a stair, is a classic location for a grand pot. Here, a stone campana-shaped urn is carved with vigorous classical detailing that catches the light well. Its unusually thick neck, or socle, is taking absolutely no chances with the most fragile area of the elegant classic garden urn.*

Earthenware containers have probably been used for growing and transporting plants since gardens began. They have hardly been surpassed, offering porosity, durability, and often good design. Almost all gardeners have used them, and only the recent advent of plastics has usurped them from commercial gardening. The gardeners of ancient Greece and Rome used earthenware pots in huge numbers. The Moorish gardeners of fourteenth-century Spain used them too, and grew fruit trees, especially figs, in terracotta pots. They were placed on terraces and in courtyards.

The terraces of sixteenth-century Italian gardens were, and often still are, enlivened by huge earthenware pots holding lemon trees. The pots, ribbed for strength, and with prominent rims to make them easier to lift and carry, were often decorated with swags of terracotta fruit and satyrs' masks in the ancient Roman manner. Containers like these are still widely made and used today.

CENTRE *The gardens at Herrenhausen in Germany, show a modern interpretation of the classical parterre, reducing it to a crisp grid of clipped box. The grid is decorated by huge terracotta pots, each containing a standard lemon tree. The pots are banded in the traditional manner, to give them greater strength, while the pronounced rims offer plenty of grip for the gardeners who have to move them around.*

Although, in the West, terracotta pots were often left unglazed, in the Islamic world, garden pots were usually splendidly decorated and glazed. In the gardens of seventeenth-century Persia and Kashmir, the glaze was called *azul*, and was the colour of blue irises. The same colour was also used for doors, grilles and water tanks. They must have looked marvellous against sun-drenched walls. Gardeners in Persia had also been using small blue and green glazed bulb bowls, designed for the water cultivation of bulbs, particularly hyacinths. When the bulbs, and the manner of growing them, reached Europe in the late sixteenth century, gardeners were fascinated. Copies of these pots were made at Delft in the Netherlands but the market was so greedy that samples of Delftware were sent to China where copies could be produced swiftly and cheaply, even if they were made of porcelain.

Though ordinary earthenware can make grand as well as humble garden pots, its somewhat rustic nature did not suit gardeners who wanted much more architectural containers. When Renaissance garden owners in sixteenth-century Rome began to collect some of the sumptuous marble urns then being excavated, the hunt was on for a material as durable as marble, but not so expensive.

ABOVE *An old farmyard trough, in crudely chiselled stone reused as a garden planter. With plenty of drainage, troughs make good places to grow alpines without having to resort to a conventional rock garden. Here, the plant is* Saxifraga × *'Tumbling Waters'.*

BELOW *A superb earthenware pot made by potter Janet Allan, has four sides made separately as slabs, and pressed into a mould, before being joined together. Here, it has been planted with a clump of sempervivums, whose brilliantly coloured stems look good against the earthy orange of the pot.*

LEFT *Old storage jars, with glazed interiors and narrow necks, are beautiful. However, it can be difficult to match a planting to their shape. They also need drainage holes, and it can be hard to repot whatever grows in them. Here, the difficulties are avoided, using the exuberant papyrus (Cyperus papyrus). It is a perfect foil to the shape of the containers.*

The hunt continued into the eighteenth century fired by the fashion for using urns as garden ornaments. Very few garden owners were rich enough to have genuine Roman marble urns in their gardens, though some did have them copied in similar material. While the rich travelled to Rome on the Grand Tour and coveted Roman antiques, it was a new discovery that made the general public lust after Roman urns. The great Warwick Vase was discovered by Gavin Hamilton at Hadrian's Villa, near Tivoli, Italy, in 1771. Brought to England and put on public display in 1778, most gardeners of the time wished for a copy.

One of the best of the cheaper substitutes for marble was made by the company begun by the Coade family. Coade 'stone', was a mix of ball clay, finely ground flint, sand, and soda-lime glass. Before firing, it was extremely flexible, first being press moulded in sections. After drying, handles, bowls, socles (stems), and decorative details were assembled to form the whole, and the seams filled in. Chased and finished, the completed object was then fired. Even huge classical statues were made and fired as entire items for four days at 1,100°C. Many Roman urns were copied, along with new-fangled designs of urns too. So tough that it hardly weathered, and never gets mossy, Coade stone was vastly popular. Catalogues of the 1760s list hundreds of urns and vases. Almost all of them were supplied with matching lids, so that they could be emptied of soil over winter, didn't fill up with water, and looked splendidly architectural in the leafless garden.

In the Orient, earthenware pots have an ancient and diverse history too. Chrysanthemums and paeonies have been grown in pots for at least 2,000 years. Bonsai have almost as long a history, and were then, and still are used for display in a special niche, or on small tables, in the main living space. Sometimes pots are placed on the verandah of a house, or on a flat stone below it. Chinese gardeners have had an exuberant approach to using containers. Huge pots often occupy bronze or stone stands in garden courtyards. They can be planted with deliberately dwarfed pines, or bamboo, or sometimes with lotus. They can even be used as carp tanks. Smaller ones are used for orchids, bonsai, and even, since their introduction, cacti. Pots were, and are, considered necessary for internal spaces — perhaps white glazed pots on low hardwood tables filled with the summer orchid (*Dendrobium goeringii*) beloved by Confucius.

Chinese containers are often brightly coloured, in contrast with Japanese ones, which use natural earth colours. A special purple terracotta is prized in China, and plant containers are often incised with poems before firing. Chinese gardeners have, for centuries used low bowls for forcing narcissus, (a Western plant that reached China before the birth of Christ), to bloom early. In the past, Chinese scholars grew *Liriope* in pots beside their desks. The plant was called the 'bookmark grass', describing the function of its long, tapering leaves.

In the West in modern times, many kinds of terracotta containers have been used for planting. Terracotta oil jars are especially popular, and echo a shape that has been in use for at least 3,000 years. The shape is so potent that contemporary potters have adapted it to make sculptural pots that are more art than function. However, the most modest containers find uses in the garden; old brown-glazed terracotta sinks, and even

ABOVE *Some recycled objects have become classics in their own right. Good Victorian chimney pots make amusing containers, with both a built-in pedestal and plenty of drainage. This one is planted up with dazzlingly pink diascias (perhaps a bit harsh with the orange brickwork behind), but they can look great fun with agapanthus, or even with some of the smaller cordylines.*

**RIGHT** *Coade stone was often used to copy antique classical urns and statuary, but it was also used in more adventurous ways. This handsome bowl, though decorated with Renaissance-influenced scrollwork, is entirely nineteenth century in shape. It makes a much better planter than many Roman urns as it is deeper, and could easily support a larger and more glamorous planting than these yellow violas.*

redundant chimneypots, can look good. Sometimes, containers have been specially designed for fashionable plants, like the familiar Victorian Burmantofts bowls and stands, glazed in murky green, which were created especially for the aspidistra. However, humble or sophisticated, nothing is more attractive in the garden than a well-aged pot.

Wood is so perishable that the only really classic containers are the great *caisses* still used at the palace of Versailles to grow orange and lemon trees, and palms. Though now conventionally called Versailles tubs, similar boxes are often seen in eighteenth-century engravings of gardens all over Europe. The sides of these great boxes were hinged to the main framework of the container so that they could be opened outwards and the soil partly excavated away from the tree's roots. This was then replaced by new soil, so the plant never had to be repotted in any radical way. It was a very successful technique, and some of the trees at Versailles were very ancient, some were even reputed to be from the thirteenth-century Chiaramontesi garden in Italy, which at one time had several thousand potted lemons and oranges.

Though modern reproduction Versailles tubs are often white, in the past they were always painted dark green, blue-black, or sometimes with the panels in grey-green, and the structure in grey. All of them make marvellous statements in formal gardens, especially if they are used in the French manner, where they flank courtyards or pathways, or are placed along the sides of a formal pool

Wooden containers were used in other garden cultures too. In Kashmir, the ancient garden of Nishat Bagh, with its blue-tiled tanks, octagonal pavilions, and central cascaded canal, had walks lined with square boxes of pomegranates and mango. In

China, gardeners often used staved tubs, which were similar to today's European half-barrel containers, in which to plant big bonsai.

Carved stone in the garden is an expensive commodity. In contemporary English gardens, stone containers are often recycled sinks or pig troughs, their new use dating from the Arts and Crafts movement of 1890s' Britain. By that date, less expensive metal containers were supplanting old stone drinking troughs and other farmyard containers. Nowadays, they look lovely planted up with saxifrages and other rockery genera, though they can look as good with much more voluptuous plantings of cosmos, and even generous amounts of lavender. These old farmyard containers acquire the patina of age and become more attractive with the passing years.

Many classic stone containers are now reproduced in reconstituted stone, which is basically concrete with additives. Though not fired, many of these containers are of excellent quality. They copy some of the best urns and other receptacles from the past and they also weather well in the garden losing their just-made look fairly rapidly. There are also good fibreglass copies, and though these often have a decorative patina applied when they are made, they do not go on to develop a real feel of age, which makes them a less attractive form of container.

Earthenware, wood and stone containers are also copied rather crudely in plastic. Plants grow in them perfectly well, though the design is often poor. The rims are sometimes turned inward in an attempt to make the pot look thicker but, in fact, there is a pitfall as these curled rims offer a perfect lair for slugs and snails. However, they are inexpensive, weatherproof and disposable.

*ABOVE Classic 1,000-year-old egg pots, often in brown glaze and decorated with a dragon, make excellent planters. Modern copies are easily available, and this one is suitably planted with the elegant bamboo Fargesia murieliae 'Simba'. Another broader-leafed bamboo that also does well in pots is Sasa veitchii. This egg pot stands against a bamboo screen; in China it would be placed against a plain whitewashed wall.*

Though lead has been used in gardens since ancient Babylon (where sheets of it were used to waterproof the planted terraces of the Hanging Gardens), it was only used for plant containers as part of the great vogue for decorative leadware that started in Europe in the early seventeenth century. By then, casting techniques were sufficiently industrialized to allow the use of lead for guttering and elegant water cisterns.

Most early lead cisterns date from around 1666, though some are earlier. Many are decorated with simple strapwork designs, sometimes enlivened with initials, roses, and, quite often, the date of casting. Some cisterns have a bronze tap near the base so that they could be drained in winter. Other cisterns are even a quarter circle in shape to enable them to fit neatly into garden corners. All the panels of the cistern were simply cast in sand boxes, and then soldered together. They supplied rainwater for both house

# METAL CISTERNS, POTS & URNS

and garden, and it was only late nineteenth-century designers like Inigo Trigg and Gertrude Jekyll who suggested their use as sumptuous garden planters.

Some of the splendid lidded lead urns found along balustrades or in use as finials at the top of gate piers or house pediments date from the seventeenth century too. The designs of many of these were based on the marble urns then still being discovered among the ruins of ancient Rome. All had lids, as did the funerary urns on which they were based. When their lids were removed during the summer, they were often planted with tulips or carnations. The lids were replaced in winter to prevent the contents from becoming waterlogged.

In their original state, most lead urns were painted off-white, more closely to resemble the marble of their originals. Both urns and rainwater tanks are still cast in lead, usually copying seventeenth- or eighteenth- century originals. Though they are now rather expensive, they make handsome planters, as the dark sheen of the lead sets off flowers and foliage to perfection.

By 1816, technological change, sparked by the Napoleonic wars, meant that iron casting had become inexpensive enough to make garden decorations rather than guns. All sorts and sizes of garden urns (as well as seats and railings) were made of this marvellous new material. As it was much cheaper than lead, artefacts made of cast iron were able to reach a huge new market, and even quite small and humble gardens were decorated with cast-iron plant pots.

In many ways, iron vases and containers were an advance because, being strong, they did not sag on their socles like earlier lead ones. However, they did rust. Cast-iron containers were always painted, though in time a great many owners came to regret this

**ABOVE** *Recycled olive oil cans have become well-established favourites, and make splendid containers for strong, simple planting such as these dazzling geraniums. Once a few drainage holes have been punched in the base, the cans hold enough soil to grow generous plants. Make sure that the drainage holes of metal containers never get blocked or the plant will drown.*

**ABOVE** *A painted cast-iron urn, almost certainly from the 1873 catalogue of A. Handyside and Co. Ltd. the famous Derbyshire foundrymen. The deep* campana *shape makes a good container especially for slightly tender plants such as this* Sphaeralcea miniata. *Be winter wary; cast-iron containers will crack if the water-logged soil inside them freezes.*

because the layers of paint eventually filled in the detailed decoration of the iron casting.

Famous foundries included companies such as A. Handyside and Co. Ltd., Carron, Saracen, and Coalbrookdale. Each company copied the designs of the other until 1842, when designs could be patented. Thereafter, many urns have registration marks on them. The output was prodigious; the Britannia Ironworks in Derbyshire offered 49 different vases. The 1875 catalogue from Coalbrookdale had 42 vases and finials. A few year later, the new magazine *Gardener's Chronicle* was selling full-page adverts for the vast ranges of cast-iron plant pots.

Popular designs for these garden features were almost entirely based on copies of various sorts of ancient Roman vessels. These included the shallow *tazza* shape, with handsome handles and fluted rim, modelled on ceremonial drinking vessels, and the deep *campana* shape based on funerary urns. The *campana*-shaped urns make much

*ABOVE Metal containers continue to be popular. Contemporary metal containers, with their strong, simple shapes and attractive surfaces, are the new classics for gardens of today . Here, the shape and colour of the hosta's waxy blue-green leaves are set off to great effect against the sheen of the galvanized metal container.*

**LEFT** *Garden containers can be used for edible plants as well as flowers. Vegetables such as the chards, seakales, even squashes and pumpkins, can make excellent container plants. Here, a green variety of kohlrabi looks good in a galvanized steel tank, though perhaps a continuously croppable brassica would be better. Try using 'Cavolo Nero', a palm tree cabbage, and a handsome plant harvested leaf by leaf.*

**RIGHT** *A handsome classic tazza-shaped container in metal provides an excellent foil for a traditional planting of tulips, violas and forget-me-nots (Myosotis). Tazza-shaped containers are shallow and apt to dry out quickly.*

better containers for plants as there is more depth in which to form good root growth.

Rules for how these classic containers should be planted were being propounded as early as 1850, when vase and vegetation had to be matched. In 1849, the magazine *The Cottage Gardener* stated that 'In every case, whether the vase be an upright Etruscan or of *tazza* form, it should be very considerably concealed by the flowers'. Cast-iron urns were commonly painted dark green, indigo green, dark brown, or bronze brown. Today, some gardeners use them sand-blasted back to brilliant metal. The urns are then given a coat of clear lacquer. They can look visually arresting, as the brilliance of the metal provides a dramatic contrast with the plants and also reflects any tumbling foliage.

Other metals such as aluminium, and various alloys, are also cast to make copies of classic urns as well as crisp contemporary containers. Even sheet steel is used to create stylish planters that can contrast strongly with interesting plantings. However, the long history of recycling domestic metalware, that today includes old olive oil cans or oil drums, can produce a new form of classic container that has an equally timeless and enchantingly rustic look. An olive oil can filled with pink geraniums is as redolent of the Mediterranean for many modern gardeners, as a copy of the Warwick vase once was.

**ABOVE** *Lead tanks like these were once used as water cisterns in courtyards and gardens. The demand for them is now high, and many lay false claim to the dates they bear and some are even fibreglass reproductions. This handsome example, with its date and random assortment of classical details, is planted up with drought-resistant osteospermums and verbenas.*

## in its setting: containers
## POWIS CASTLE, WALES

1 Each tall, narrow niche holds a dramatic pot on a stand. The planting shown here features pelargoniums and tropaeolums. The pots need watering several times a day during the summer, but the luxuriance of their planting is unsurpassed. Extravagant spirals of box topiary would, perhaps, be an excellent alternative.

2 The extraordinary terraces of Powis Castle, caught in evening light, show how dramatic topiary, statuary, and huge lead urns can be when allied with imagination, wealth, and an exciting site. Nevertheless, even in a tiny garden, a well placed feature can add tremendous drama.

The ancient castle of Powis, near Welshpool, was built by the princes of Powys (sic) over 800 years ago. They owned it until the reign of William III, when it passed to the earls of Rochford who transformed it into a great country house. The first earl began the garden terraces as a way of giving a glamorous casing to the bare south-east facing rock on which his castle stood. They were created as a splendid framework for statuary and containers for the very rarest and most tender of plants.

The terraces were finished by 1722, and are nearly 152m (500ft) long, linked by flights of steps worthy of an Italian palace. Yews were planted along the uppermost level in the 1720s, and may have been trimmed as narrow obelisks. Now they are vast cushions of blackish green, and contrast well with the rose coloured brick of the terraces.

The topmost terrace has been given an extraordinary series of handsome classical niches, alternating with panelled sections of wall. The niches have probably always held lushly planted containers. Terracotta and Coade stone containers decorate all the balustrades, or stand grandly on the linking staircases. Though the planting in the huge terracotta urns in the niches changes from season to season, one of the most successful is a combination of artemisias, soft blue *Salvia patens* and sprays of lemon verbena (*Lippia citriodora*). The base of the walls, where troupes of peacocks carefully pose, is smothered in the billowing silvery lace of *Artemisia* 'Powis Castle'.

3 Terracotta pots with basket-weave patterning like this have been popular since at least the 1820s, and can still be found. This one, on one of the lower balustrades at Powis Castle, has a generous planting of several sorts of fuchsia, one of the specialities of the garden. Narrow flowered varieties, of which 'Thalia' is one of the best, are especially suitable for narrow pots like this.

**4** The Orangery was moved to its present site on the lowest terrace in the early twentieth century. Inside, marble busts of Roman emperors are luxuriously draped with ferns and passion-flowers. Outside, the Orangery is flanked by vast, almost black, yew hedges and borders filled with pink daylilies (*Hemerocallis*) and the extraordinary, rich red *Crocosmia* 'Lucifer'. The terracotta pots hold clipped citrus trees.

135

# THE WORKING GARDEN

# PRODUCE OF THE WORKING GARDEN

The kitchen garden and its products have long been essential to people around the world. For centuries, it was the only type of garden for most people, as before the nineteenth century, it was usually only the rich who could afford the luxury of gardens for flowers alone. The less fortunate relied on their plots for food and medicinal herbs and grew flowers in between. In the working garden the well-being of the plants is paramount, and to ensure this, some design is necessary, even if only the shape and size of the planting beds.

The distinction between working and pleasure garden did not arise until the Renaissance, when new plants arrived from the Americas in such numbers that many had no obvious use as food or medicinal material, so were grouped together as merely decorative. Even then, the mixing of food crops and flowers persisted in grand gardens in Scotland and Scandinavia well into the eighteenth century, and in cottagers' gardens in Europe and North America for another hundred years.

The working garden has its own set of classic features such as bell-jars, beehives, potting sheds, and rhubarb forcers. A strong design structure is essential if the garden is to produce good crops, and the design can make the garden look good too. Climbing crops can be grown up trelliswork or cane obelisks, or over arbours. Top fruit, particularly apples and pears, can be trained and pruned into decorative shapes that control the trees' size and increase their productivity. Bush fruit, like currants and gooseberries, can be pruned to make attractive standards. Even fruit cages, which keep the blackbirds from the strawberries and raspberries, can be stylish. And the potting shed can be a romantic place of retreat as well as a storage place for implements. Working gardens should be a pleasure to be in, and a source of delight as well as good things for the table.

OVERLEAF *These handsome skeps, or straw beehives, in a Belgian garden are re-creations of those common until the late eighteenth century, when wooden ones, filled with frames for the bees to store their honey, became more widespread. In straw or rush hives, the colonies often had to be destroyed to obtain the crop.*

RIGHT *In this French kitchen garden, at Cordes-sur-Ciel, the stout posts supporting the tomatoes are a visual feature in their own right. In the background more posts make a pergola over a shaded pathway, as well as a platform for drying corn. The plant among the tomatoes is Nankin perilla (Perilla frutescens crispa).*

BELOW *Vertical emphasis is as important a design feature in the working garden as it is among flowers and shrubs. Here, strongly built obelisks of bamboo are already half smothered in runner beans. Climbing French beans can look even more dramatic, and non-bush forms of courgette will climb energetically too.*

LEFT *In the kitchen garden of the ancient Priory d'Orsan, in France, low wattle edging holds up a raised bed filled with orange pumpkins. Wattle-edged beds are shown in many illustrations well into the sixteenth century.*

# PLANTING UP THE POTAGER

The French word *potager* means kitchen garden, and though many French vegetable patches are visually satisfying mixes of delicious things, the present-day usage in the English language has come to mean something with more pretension, though still offering a good way of integrating flowers and vegetables. The potager is a particularly useful sort of garden for gardeners with little space: in the best , fruits, vegetables, herbs and flowers combine into a seductive and productive mix. Form is given to the garden by decorative features such as wire-work or bamboo obelisks for beans, and augmented by espalier fruit trees pruned into elaborate shapes. Great examples include the potager at the Château de Villandry, in the Loire valley, France, where the decorative possibilities of fruit and vegetables are taken to their limits, and are very lovely. Even in lesser gardens, when done with flair, potagers can look remarkably pretty and still provide good fruit and vegetables in abundance.

In North America, particularly in some of the communal inner-city gardens, there are serious potagers, filled with food crops as well as flowers. These working gardens are a world away from the decorator-inspired gardens often seen in Britain. They have given rise to some of the most vital garden designs of today.

The gardens of ancient Rome were quite as exuberant, and some of those excavated at Pompeii suggest that even gardens of grand houses had luxuriant beds of salads and vegetables. It is thought that *triclinia* (turf, brick and masonry seats), shaded by vines, were set among a mixture of artichokes, lettuces, chards, violets and lilies. The tradition of mixing flowers and vegetables was upheld in modest gardens well into the seventeenth century. In *The Scots Gard'ner* of 1683 John Reid describes mixes of roses and cabbages, and sets them in a parterre of box and holly. The cottage garden so beloved by nineteenth-century garden painters and writers was the continuation of that tradition.

Potagers look best when strongly formal in layout, either in the ancient plan of four squares that harks back to the very earliest gardens of all, or with a pattern of beds 1.2 to 1.8m (4 to 6ft) across. That width allows the gardener to sow, maintain and crop the beds from the paths, and so avoid standing on the earth. The beds should be as long as the gardener needs for the design, or as the kitchen demands. Paths should be 90cm or 1.2m (3 or 4ft) wide to give easy access to the beds, and through the garden. They should be of grass or grit, or a similar finish.

The stronger the design the better the potager will look in winter, when only a few beds will still have crops in them. To emphasize this, the beds need edging. Medieval gardeners used miniature wattle fences to hold back the soil, and these have seen a resurgence in popularity. Renaissance gardens more commonly had painted boards, stone edging, or bricks. Early eighteenth-century beds were often edged in box. By the nineteenth century, edgings had become softer plantings of alpine strawberries, herbs such as chives, parsley and silver thyme, or salads like purslane and cress.

To enhance the formality, vegetable climbers, such as beans and squashes, are an excellent choice to clamber over a central feature. An arbour of wood or metal over a bench, or a rough pavilion at the crossing of the garden paths can also make delightful features. The framework should be covered with black pigeon netting to let the climbers twine easily. An arbour gives the cook somewhere peaceful to sit, to sniff the herbs, and survey an elegant garden with standard gooseberries and currants dripping with fruit, its beds filled with salads, and its espaliers burdened with apples and pears.

RIGHT *A potager with a four-part division is a design that links back directly to the very earliest gardens of Mesopotamia. The central water feature makes the link even stronger. Here, the design is emphasized by low box hedges, topiary cones, and durable brick paths. The enclosing hedges are decorated with topiary balls.*

Potting sheds are one of the most alluring and romantic of working garden classics, though they are emptier now and smaller than they used to be. In the days when gardens had full-time gardeners they held a clutter of implements, and a miscellany of other gardening necessities such as blinds, cloches, paper frames, bags for figs and grapes, derris puffers, nets for catching peaches, apple trays, numerous shapes of earthenware pots and specimen pans.

One reason why potting sheds are emptier now is that in the past there were many more varieties of hand implements such as rakes, scythes and spades and many were specialized for certain tasks. Most were made by local blacksmiths. Each region of a European country had many types, and variants within the type. North American implements were more standardized and often followed Dutch and German styles. Many country junk shops still have good stocks of old garden implements, and because many were well made, they can still be used. It always feels good to use an implement that has some age behind it, and has been used by generations of other gardeners.

# THE LURE OF THE POTTING SHED

*RIGHT Even the pansies at the window are in old earthenware pots in this potting shed where sieves, cart wheels, and old garden implements decorate the exterior. Apart from the wheel and weathervane, most of the other items would once have been stored indoors, the implements carefully cleaned and oiled to prevent them from rusting.*

*RIGHT A good way to make the most prosaic potting shed look romantic is to smother it with vegetation. Here ivy and roses are used, but hops and clematis would be good too. The idea of a quiet afternoon in the garden is emphasized by a comfortable nineteenth-century bench amid ground elder.*

*FAR RIGHT Hanging on the extreme right of the shelf in this picturesque tangle of old-fashioned implements (all now collectable), is a mattock, one of the oldest types. Roman gardeners used a two-pronged version called a bidens. Variants are still used to loosen soil and cut roots all over the world, though they are now rarely seen in Europe.*

Handles were often of hazel wood which is so springy and tough that it had a multitude of other uses such as hurdles, wattle, springs for bird traps, poles and rake handles. Most metal spades are Victorian or later; before that spades had metal-shod wooden blades. Scythes also had a place in the potting shed. Lawns were usually cut only once a fortnight even in high summer, for the grass had to be long enough to catch on the scythe's blade. Scything left a slightly uneven effect that was much cherished.

Potting sheds once contained mattocks, a dozen different sorts of rake, compost, seed trays, towels, dibbers, twine, and of course, hosepipes. These were important. Hoses were used to water gardens from the early eighteenth century. At first, they were made of leather, carefully stitched, but prone to rot and leak. With the discovery of gutta-percha, a type of latex, in the nineteenth century, exciting new hosepipes made of the brown rubber substance began to save hours of gardeners' time and energy, although the old-fashioned leather hose was still available in the 1870s.

Medieval watering cans were made of earthenware. There were various shapes, from spouted jugs with crude roses, to bell-shapes with perforated bottoms and a narrow neck that could be closed by the gardener's thumb to regulate the flow of water. Metal cans were made from the late seventeenth century, some even had two spouts for watering two pots at once, but surviving cans are mostly eighteenth century. Copper was the most favoured material, and some old French cans have considerable elegance. The

great age of the watering can was the nineteenth century, when a huge range was marketed. Cans with hooped-tube handles running from top to bottom are usually French, while British watering cans had handles of flattened strip metal. Galvanized watering cans were first made in the late nineteenth century. Haws, a British firm that began in the nineteenth-century and still exists, made the best. Its products are easily dated by the brass plate riveted to the body of the can.

Potting sheds also sheltered big implements like wheelbarrows over winter. Ancient barrows often did not have wheels, just a frame with a pair of handles at each end, which needed two gardeners to carry it. Flat barrows like these are shown in Roman mosaics, and remained current into the eighteenth century. Wheeled barrows were in use a century earlier, the main frame often made of springy ash wood, with an elm body. Old barrows have spoked wooden wheels with an iron rim.

The shed is still the place for the mower. Lawnmowers are an early nineteenth-century British invention, first commercially marketed in 1830. Before that, scythes were

the only way of cutting grass. The first mowers are all variants of the cylinder mower. The lawnmower created a new means of judging the perfect lawn: stripes. By 1856, lawns were becoming less expensive to own and manage, for the mowing machines made their maintenance much easier. The most popular model still needed two men to operate it; one to push, one to pull. Large establishments had horse-drawn mowers, and the horses wore large leather shoes to stop their iron-shod hooves ruining the lawn's surface.

The British company Greens introduced the first effective one-person lawnmower at a cost of five shillings. A lighter model for ladies, called the 'Parvum Miraculum', was

*BELOW Some splendid galvanised watering cans: the one in front with the handle forming three quarters of a circle is a French design, and has a spout for watering pots. The others follow English patterns, and have lost their brassware roses.*

a shilling dearer. By 1862, there were several types of lawnmower and controversy raged over which was best, rather as it does today, giving rise to a massive correspondence in all the gardening magazines.

Rollers had been necessary for lawns and bowling greens since the seventeenth century. Early ones had stone cylinders, a type that lasted well. Cast-iron rollers are mostly early nineteenth century or later. They come as single or double cylinder forms (double makes them easier to turn without ripping the turf), often with rounded edges to the cylinders, and a balance handle. The handle was connected to weights inside the hollow rollers, so that when not in use the handle stood upright. Many manufacturers made them, though the basic product was almost identical. They had fancy names for such humble things: 'Court Royal', 'Marlborough', and the 'Marylebone'.

The potting shed is a great source of delight and solace. Every garden should have at least a shack – a lesser pavilion and quite as much fun – to spend time in. Commercial sheds can easily be personalized. Paint them in your colours, or cover them with trellis and climbers, or let ivy turn them into a snug retreat.

*LEFT Wheelbarrows have looked like this since the seventeenth century. This late nineteenth-century example with a good, sturdy shape, has had its original iron-rimmed and wooden-spoked wheel replaced with a rubber-tyred version, which is much more comfortable for the gardener to use.*

*ABOVE Rollers with balance handles were once common in every suburban garden, and still exist in large quantities. The decorative metal circle between the shafts of the handle contains the name of the maker and the style of the roller. The frame base behind once had a glazed lid, and was used to grow, among many other fruits and vegetables, melons, cucumbers and early peas.*

Roman gardeners may have had some way for forcing plants into early flower or fruit; a verse of Martial, the Roman poet, implies that he had early cherries (just introduced to Europe from Anatolia) and peaches. However, the skill seems to have vanished, though there are European references to heated garden buildings with ordinary windows being used as orangeries from the fifteenth century. Little more was attempted until the middle of the sixteenth century.

The process was, at least partly, dependent on the use of glass, whether as a bell-jar (a one-piece cloche) or in sheet form to glaze boxes or frames. In the mid-sixteenth century glass became affordable to use for garden buildings, but even then, only in very grand establishments. Lord Burleigh had a purpose-built orangery by 1561, but it took

# FORCING PLANTS INTO LIFE

**FAR LEFT** *A row of glass bell-jars, increasingly hard to find at this size, are being used to force salad plants. Identical glasses have been used at least since the late seventeenth century in Europe and North America. Modern reproductions are often too small to do much more than protect the youngest of plants.*

**LEFT** *This well-blanched seakale has been growing for a month or more beneath a terracotta forcing pot. The lid allows the gardener to check on its progress. The pale leaves and stalks taste like a very superior cabbage.*

another 250 years before sheet glass became inexpensive enough to risk in the average garden in a full-sized greenhouse or frame.

The bell-jar seems to have been among the first pieces of forcing equipment widely used. A sketch of 1659 by the gentleman-gardener John Evelyn for *Elysium Brittanicum*, a book that he never completed, shows one of the first. The bell-jars he drew were used to force salads, protect strawberries, and even to keep picked cherries fresh. By the end of the 1840s, bell-jars had a new function; city air was so sulphurous that new viola hybrids died as soon as they were planted out. City gardeners could only grow them beneath bell-jars. In France, gardeners even had neatly woven straw covers to put over the jars on chilly nights. Bell-jars were still in use in the early part of the twentieth century and are now being reproduced for nostalgic gardeners.

Bell-jars were also often used on hot-beds, where they were placed over each young plant. A big disadvantage was that the heat rising from the dung created water vapour, and the atmosphere beneath the glass became extremely humid. In large establishments, an apprentice gardener was employed to prop the glasses up on pieces of twig, to give much-needed ventilation during daylight hours.

Bell-jars, even of the thickest, greenest glass, are fragile. Metal-framed lantern cloches, or handlights, as they are also known, with pyramid-shaped tops, and four 'walls' that slotted together beneath, were stronger, and much more expensive. Several sets of walls could be stacked on top of one another to make frames for quite tall plants. They are extremely effective, and are now so much sought after that copies are being made, though they are expensive and do not have the weight and size of the originals. Lantern cloches were also illustrated by John Evelyn as early as 1659, but most survivors date from the nineteenth century. The extensive Coalbrookdale Foundry catalogue of 1875 shows the now rare octagonal cloches, but the square lantern cloches were made well into the twentieth century.

**LEFT** *This Victorian lantern cloche has the same function as a bell-jar, except that ventilation is very much easier. The top can be used without any wall sections, or with several wall sets to make a taller version. Though they were cast in large numbers, original examples are surprisingly rare, but it is possible to find reproductions.*

Other classic forcers are the great earthenware 'chimney pots' with lids, that were used for forcing rhubarb and seakale. Rhubarb forcers are taller than those for seakale. Both sorts were made by the Sankey, Bulwell Potteries in Nottingham. They kept plants in the dark, blanching the stalks and supposedly improving the flavour. Fermenting manure piled around the pots kept the plants warm. Most are nineteenth century. Indeed, seakale was only brought into cultivation in the late eighteenth century. Before then, the wild plants of the sea shore seem to have been enough to supply the markets.

# OF BIRDS & BEES

ABOVE *In northern Europe, where spring comes late, bee skeps were often set into niches in south-facing walls to give the colonies extra warmth. Bee skeps are frequently found in seventeenth- and eighteenth-century gardens. The shelter of the niches gave the bee colonies a longer season of activity, and so better yields of honey.*

The cottage garden fantasy – in which every cottage garden was filled lavender, myrtle, cabbages and roses, where doves cluttered thatched roofs, and bees buzzed among the gnarled but laden fruit trees – began to appear in the European press in the 1840s, and 20 years later in North America. However far from the real life of the rural poor, the image was remarkably powerful. It gained in popularity throughout the nineteenth century, as more of the population of both continents became exclusively urban. Town gardeners yearned for orchards with ducks and chickens, or gardens with rows of bee hives by the hedge.

Ducks and chickens really need their own quarters, but bees are easily integrated into the working garden. First kept as a source of honey, the only sweetener until sugar became expensively available in medieval times, bees were cultivated by the ancient Egyptians. They, like the ancient Greeks, had hives of woven straw or reeds. Roman beekeepers had cork bark hives, woven osier hives, and brick hives, as well as good lists of bee-friendly flowers. Looking after bees was a female occupation, and remained so in Europe into the seventeenth century. By 1670, honey bees had been taken to North America and every settler had one or two hives. The eighteenth century saw the introduction of protective gear for beekeepers, as well as smokers to keep bees quiet. A quiescent colony allowed honey to be harvested without destroying the insects themselves.

ABOVE *A wooden beehive makes a splendid feature among flowers or herbs. Bee-friendly plants in the working garden include lemon balm (Melissa officinalis), marjorams, all sorts of mint and thyme, and many sorts of bean. Bees are essential for good crops from orchard fruits too.*

LEFT *North American gardens often have imaginative features like this red-painted bird house in a contemporary garden designed by Walter Oehme and James van Sweden. In European working gardens, the range of bird houses is smaller, and they are mostly designed for pigeons.*

Home-produced honey is delicious, but a hive of bees ensures pollination that is essential for all bean crops, as well as marrows and squashes. Bees also guarantee that the top fruit sets well. Wooden beehives were produced in huge numbers in the nineteenth century, though straw skeps have never entirely fallen out of use.

Doves and pigeons have a slightly more ambivalent role in the garden, adoring, as they do, young cabbages and salad crops. That was fine when they provided a succulent crop of squabs (young birds just in feather) for the table. Their possession was often the right of the feudal landlord, and the tower 'doo'cot' or 'columbarium' was a significant garden building and a highly decorative feature on estates in sixteenth-century Scotland, and southern France. The pigeon house on a pole became a fashionable garden feature in the late 1800s, as many garden catalogues of that date show. Designed to hold only a few pairs of birds, poles were often 4.5m (15ft) high to stop rats or squirrels making off with eggs and chicks. Usually made of deal, they are traditionally painted dark green or white.

# in its setting: the working garden
## LES QUATRE VENTS, CANADA

On the shores of the St Lawrence estuary near Quebec City in Canada is the kitchen garden of Les Quatre Vents. Though this area of the farm has been a vegetable garden since the 1930s, it has been re-created as a potager since the 1980s by its owners Mr & Mrs Frank Cabot. The soil was too thin for good growing, so spruce logs were used to create raised beds containing deeper soil. The layout of the beds was dictated by the gently sloping site.

The basic plan is formal and the individual beds are edged with marigolds to emphasize their shape. There are paths running through each of the beds, for cultivating and harvesting the crop. Some of the beds contain different sorts of brassica, some edible, some not, set out in decorative schemes. Rows of standard pruned apples line the main axis, and obelisks of bamboo support luxuriant runner beans. Fruit cages protect their crops, particularly the white-fruited raspberries, against raiders, and delightful scarecrows may (or may not) scare the crows. Flowers for cutting, particularly Pacific hybrid delphiniums, sweet peas and Shirley poppies, add generous colour.

The rest of the garden at Les Quatre Vents covers 8 hectares, (20 acres) and offers an amalgam of the garden styles of two countries, with areas that contain canals, pools and allées in the French manner, and a white garden and rose gardens in the English. All the areas are unified by two main axes that run through the whole garden and end in wide views of the Lawrentian countryside.

1

2

**2** The bamboo pyramid awaits the first twining shoot of the beans. Bamboo is so smooth that the first shoots sometimes need tying in until they are tightly coiled enough to get a proper grip.

**3** The building among the trees was once the old dairy and laundry. Now converted to a marvellous potting shed, it overlooks the garden's fruit trees, including the apple 'Fameuse', beds of squashes and tomatoes, and well-grown cabbages. There is also a meadow garden, which is filled with lupins, oriental poppies, filipendulas, and the invasive but very pretty *Campanula rapunculoides*.

**1** The kitchen garden at Les Quatre Vents is designed as much for visual pleasure as for its production. The wide central grass path is bordered by rectangular beds edged with French marigolds. The scarecrows are made and clothed by Mrs Cabot, and while adding to the visual excitement, also protect beds of strawberries.

**4** The blue-green foliage of cabbages (several of the 'January King' types) are contrasted cleverly with drifts of blue-purple delphiniums. The kitchen garden is at its best in September, when the crops are mature. The Cabots find it one of the most visually rewarding areas of the garden.

151

# SUPPLIERS

For some of the general materials for garden features, especially new or second-hand building materials, garden antiques, tradesmen and craftsmen, have a look at local trades directories, or the Yellow Pages. Your local Development Agency will also have lists of sculptors, potters, metal workers and so on. Not all of them will have time to carry out a small-scale commission, but many will jump at the chance to do a big one.

Another increasingly important resource for finding garden features is the internet. There are a number of general directory sites that might be useful for tracking down special items. 'The Directory' lists all sorts of new garden buildings, from sheds to poultry houses, from a large number of suppliers in Britain, Europe, North America, and Australia. Find it at: www.gardenbuildings.com/directory.

Have a look at www.salvoweb.co.uk another excellent directory site if you want to find suppliers for antique paviours, bricks and timber, as well as garden urns and statuary. It lists a few North American and European sources, but is mostly British based.

However, a search using any of the search engines will reveal all sorts of interesting sites.

There turn out to be societies devoted to the study of sundials, antique lawnmowers, and very much more. It is also important to remember that many firms producing excellent garden features, and especially many craftsmen, are not yet on the web.

Some suppliers and makers of garden features produce a wide range. Most suppliers need to cater for a huge variety of garden tastes, so among gnomes, and statues only very approximately based on Michelangelo's 'David', might be that one perfect classic feature for your garden. Good hunting.

## WATER

*Pools and ponds are such enormously popular and satisfying garden features that there are large numbers of companies supplying equipment, pond liners, pumps and plants. There are also many contractors happy to build your miroir d'eau or simple frog pond for you. It does not matter what holds the water in. The most important thing for the look of any water feature is the way that the margin is treated.*

### BRIDGES
Coulson's Bridges
Coulson's Laminations
Broom Hill
Polstead
Suffolk CO6 5AQ
Tel: 01206 262387
Fax: 01206 263073
Email: sales@coulsonbridges.co.uk

### WALL MASKS
The Landscape Ornament Company
Long Barn
Patney
Devizes
Wiltshire SN10 3RB
Tel: 01380 840533
Fax: 01380 848189
Email: loc@balston.co.uk

Green Man
Citrus Tree Court
Hoar Park Village
Ansley
Nuneaton
Warks CV10 0QU
Tel: 02476 395421

## PLANT SUPPORTS

### OBELISKS
*Try joiners, timber merchants and metal workers and also:*

Haddonstone
The Forge House
East Haddon
Northampton NN6 8DB
Tel: 01604 770711
Fax: 01604 770027
**www.haddonstone.co.uk**

### PERGOLAS AND ARCHES
*These are almost always made individually. It is possible to use the pole and rope solution or get a builder to use reproduction Roman columns. However, the nicest pergolas are stone or brick built and a local builder should be able to find local materials to match your house.*

Outdoor Interiors
PO Box 40
Woking
Surrey GU22 7YU
Tel: 01483 727888
Fax: 01483 727828

### ROPES
W R Outhwaite & Son Ropemakers
Town Foot
Hawes
North Yorkshire DL8 3NT
Tel: 01969 667487
Fax: 01969 667576
Email: sales@ropemakers.co.uk

### TRELLISWORK AND PANELS
Anthony de Grey Trellises
Broadhinton Yard
77a North Street
London SW4 0HQ
Tel: 020 7738 8866
Fax: 020 7498 9075
www.anthonydegrey.com

Christopher Winder Joinery
Court Lodge Farm
Hinxhill
Ashford
Kent TN25 5NR
Tel: 01233 625204
Fax: 01233 621155

## WILLOW

English Hurdle
Curload
Stoke St Gregory
Taunton
Somerset TA3 6JD
Tel: 01823 698418
Fax: 01823 698859
Email: hurdle@enterprise.net
www.hurdle.co.uk

# WALLS, GATES, PATHS AND STEPS

## GATES

Jardine Essex
108-112 Westmoor Street
Charlton
London SE7 8NQ
Tel: 020 8858 6110
Fax: 020 8763 9812

## GRILLES

Freegate Metal Products Limited
Freegate Mill
Cowling
Nr Keighley
West Yorkshire BD22 0DJ
Tel & Fax: 01535 632723
Email: freegate@mywebpage.net
www.mywebpage.net/freegate

## DECKING

UK Decks
PO Box 1234
Sheffield S11 7XT
Tel: 01142 631500
www.ukdecks.com

## PAVIOURS

G. O'Brien & Sons Ltd
Cleadon Lane
East Boldon
Tyne & Wear NE36 0JA
Tel: 01915 374332

# TOPIARY

*An increasing number of companies grow their own or import topiary from the surprising number of Dutch and Italian companies that specialize in it. It is possible to buy full-grown peacocks, estrade shapes, obelisks, globes, and others. Many European companies have regular deliveries to Britain, so check with your garden centre. It is also possible to find yew and box hedging.*

## PREGROWN TOPIARY

The Topiary Specialist
Swannington
Norwich
Norfolk NR9 5NW
Tel: 01603 261488
Fax: 01603 8716678

The Knot Garden
Heydon Lane
Wood Dalling
Norwich
Norfolk NR11 6SA
Tel: 01263 587051

## TOPIARY FRAMES

Capital Garden Products
Gibbs Reed Barn
Pashley Road
Ticehurst
E. Sussex TM5 7HE
Tel: 01580 201092
Fax: 01580 201093
Email: sales@capital.garden.com

# CENTREPIECES

## LEAD GARDEN STATUARY

The Bulbeck Foundry
Reach Road
Burwell
Cambs. CB5 0AH
Tel: 01638 743153

## SUNDIALS AND ARMILLARY SPHERES

*A full list of almost all UK makers can be found at:*
www.sundials.co.uk/makers.htm

Brookbrae Ltd
St. Leonard Road
London SW14 7NQ
Tel: 020 8876 9238
Fax: 020 8878 9415

David Brown
21 Radstock Road
Midsomer Norton
Bath BA3 2AJ

Chapel Sundials
The Old Chapel
Newfound
Basingstoke
Hants RG23 7HH

Connoisseur Sun Dials
Lane End
Strefford
Craven Arms
Shropshire SY7 8DE
Tel: 01588 672126

David Gulland
The Old Coach House
Rotchell Road
Dumfries DG2 7SP
Tel: 01387 251492

Sally Hersh
Sycamores Studio
School Lane
Lodsworth  Petworth,
W. Sussex GU28 9DH
Tel: 01798 861248
Fax: 01798 861355
Email: info@sallyhersh.com

Harriet James
Staverton
North Trowbridge
Wilts BA14 6PB
Tel: 01225 782561
Email: sunnydials@compuserve.com

Westwood Dials
White House Farm
New Hall Lane
Nr Maldon
Essex CM9 6PJ
Tel: 01621 740599
Fax: 01277 227665
Email: westwood.dials@virgin.net

## JAPANESE LANTERNS

*Still produced in huge numbers in Japan they can be found in bronze as well as granite. Some reach this country. It is possible to find good reproductions but there are terrible ones too. Beware.*

Granite Connection Ltd
East View Terrace
Langley Mill
Nottinghamshire NG16 4DF
Tel: 01773 533090
www.graniteconnection.co.uk

## OTHER LANTERNS

Omniglow Ltd
Netherhampton Road
Salisbury
Wiltshire SP7 8PU
Tel: 01722 744737

Haddonstone
The Forge House
East Haddon
Northampton NN6 8DB
Tel: 01604 770711
Fax: 01604 770027
www.haddonstone.co.uk

## 'STONE' STATUARY AND URNS

*Italian companies are still making good semi-baroque garden statuary in some quantity. Much of it is machine carved and lacks the finesse of the real thing. Still, it is very, very much cheaper and can look fine at a distance and once weathered. The reproduction companies copy some good features. An urn is almost always an easier choice than a statue and you can put plants in it too.*

Chilstone
Victoria Park
Fordcombe Road
Langton Green
Tunbridge Wells
Kent TN3 0RE
Tel: 01892 740866
Fax: 01892 740249
Email: chilstone@hndl.demon.co.uk
www.greatbritain.co.uk/chilstone

Pyramidion
PO Box 3
Hay on Wye
Herefordshire HR3 5YA
Tel: 01497 847171
Fax: 01497 847063
Email: sales@pyramidion.com

Haddonstone
The Forge House
East Haddon
Northampton NN6 8DB
Tel: 01604 770711
Fax: 01604 770027
www.haddonstone.co.uk

Jardinique
Old Park Farm
Kings Hill
Beech
Alton
Hampshire GU34 4AW
Tel: 01420 560055
Fax: 01420 560050
Email: enquiries@jardinique.co.uk
www.jardinique.co.uk

Triton Castings
Torbay Road
Castle Cary
Somerset BA7 7DT
Tel: 01963 351653
Fax: 01963 351656
Email: sales@tritoncastings.com
www.tritoncastings.com

## PAVILIONS AND GAZEBOS

*Though there are some fine retreats to be had off the shelf some are so expensive that it is worth checking out what a local joiner would charge for making something comparable. However, the following companies have some interesting structures.*

Garden Architecture
PO Box 7470
Sutton Coldfield B74 4TW
Tel: 0121 353 0345
Fax: 0121 353 0245
Email:
enquiries@woodworkshop.co.uk
www.woodworkshop.co.uk

Jacksons Fencing
31 Stowting Common
Ashford
Kent TN25 6BN
Tel: 0800 41 43 43
www.jacksons-fencing.co.uk

Pinelog Ltd
Riverside Works
Bakewell
Derbyshire DE45 1GS
Tel: 01629 814481
www.pinelog.co.uk

Machin Designs
Faverdale
Darlington
Co. Durham DL3 0PW
Tel: 01325 360776
email: machin@amdega.co.uk
www.design.zebra.co.uk/machin/holding

Courtyard Designs
Suckley
Worcester WR6 5EH
Tel: 01886 884640
Fax: 01886 884444

# SEATING

*Essential in every garden, seating is one of the easiest fields in which to find classics. There is not much point in looking for antiques. Even when they exist they need a lot of restoration. Many classics are reproduced and some of the more interesting joinery companies produce some good designs of their own. Pine seats painted in a colour and well maintained can easily last for twenty years and more, so do not deprive yourself of an opportunity for colour by buying teak or some other tropical hard wood.*

## ADIRONDACKS

*Hardly produced in Europe, there are huge numbers of American joinery businesses making them. These are often in kit form and in flat-pack and shipped internationally. Try these web based ones:*

Adirondack Wood Products
174 Larkspur Road
Stamford
CT 06903
USA
Tel: (203) 322 4518
Email: planter01@aol.com
www.adirondackwoodproducts.com

The Adirondack Source
3959 N. Buffalo Road
Orchard Park
NY 14127
USA
Tel & Fax: (888) 484 0178
*Email: sales@rlwoodworks.com*
www.rlwoodworks.com

## CAST-IRON

*Antique seats can occasionally be found at auction or at antique dealers. A number of iron founders are still casting from old moulds and so there is no particular advantage in having an old casting. Check your local directory.*

Bruton Cast Ltd
Unit 1
Station Road
Bruton
Somerset BA10 0EH
Tel: 01749 813266
www.brutoncast.com

Freegate-Metal Products Limited
Freegate Mill
Cowling
Nr Keighley
West Yorkshire BD22 0DJ
Tel & Fax: 01535 632723
Email: freegate@mywebpage.net
www.mywebpage.net/freegate

## WROUGHT-IRON

Christopher Hartnoll
Little Bray House
Brayford
Nr Barnstaple
Devon EX32 7QG
Tel: 01598 710295
http://pages.zoom.co.uk/hartnoll

## WIREWORK

Matthew Eden
Pickwick End
Corsham
Wiltshire SN13 0BJ
Tel: 01249 713335

## STONE

Haddonstone
The Forge House
East Haddon
Northampton NN6 8DB
Tel: 01604 770711
Fax: 01604 770027
www.haddonstone.co.uk

# CONTAINERS

*Garden centres are beginning to stock increasingly large and sometimes good garden pots. There are even companies that reproduce some of the classics of the nineteenth century. However, your local potter may be itching to try something big that ties the kiln up for days but which will make a big splash in your own garden.*

## VERSAILLES TUBS

*No-one seems to be making tubs in either large sizes or with sides authentically hinged. However, a local joiner and blacksmith may be able to put something interesting together. In cities they are hard to find. Alternatively try:*

Designs in Wood
Cressbrook Mill
Nr Buxton
Derbyshire SK17 8SY
Tel: 01298 872254
www.designsinwood.co.uk

## TERRACOTTA POTS

Richard Charters
Harehope Forge Pottery
Alnwick
Newcastle NE66 2DW
Tel: 01668 217347
Fax: 01665 510624
Email: charters@tagish.co.uk
www.tag.co.uk/harehope

Pots and Pithoi
The Barns
East Street
Turners Hill
West Sussex RH10 4QQ
Tel: 01342 714793

Teast Trading
Providence Place
6 Bellevue Road
Wivenhoe
Essex CO7 9LE

Studio Pots
Catriona McLean
Sanquhar House
Sanquhar
Dumfriesshire DG9 6JL
Tel: 01659 50282
Fax: 01659 58050
Email: catrionamclean@dial.pipex.com

## LEAD CONTAINERS

Steven C Markham
Unit 3
Little Shellwood Farm
Clayhill Road
Leigh
Surrey RH2 8PA
Tel: 01306 611663
Fax: 01306 611435
Email: scmleadwork@easynet.co.uk
www.stephencmarkham.co.uk

Redfields Ltd
Redlane Nursery
Churt Road
Headley
Hants GU35 8SR
Tel & Fax: 01428 714638
Email: paul@redfields.co.uk

Heveningham Collection
East Stoke Farmhouse
Stoke Charity
Winchester
Hants SO21 3PL
Tel: 01962 761777
www.heveningham.co.uk

## PLASTIC CONTAINERS

*Garden centres seem unable to supply good plastic pots. American gardeners are better looked after. However, some companies produce extremely good fibreglass containers though even the 'aged' ones do not develop a proper patina. On the other hand they do not need protection in the winter.*

Capital Garden Products
Gibbs Reed Barn
Pashley Road
Ticehurst
East Sussex TM5 7HE
Tel: 01580 201092
Fax: 01580 201093
Email: sales@capital.garden.com

Chilstone
Victoria Park
Fordcombe Road
Langton Green
Tunbridge Wells
Kent TN3 0RE
Tel: 01892 740866
Fax: 01892 740249
Email: chilstone@hndl.demon.co.uk
www.greatbritain.co.uk/chilstone

Heveningham Collection
East Stoke Farmhouse
Stoke Charity
Winchester
Hants SO21 3PL
Tel: 01962 761777
www.heveningham.co.uk

Cranbourne Stone
West Orchard
Shaftesbury
Dorset SP7 0LG
Tel: 01258 472685
Fax: 01258 471251
www.cranbournestone.com

## CERAMIC

*Importers of Oriental goods are a good source though too often like ceramic elephants seats – fun but not classics.*

Oriental Ceramics
Bromsborough Heath Business Park
Bromsborough
Ledbury
Herefordshire HR8 1PG
Tel: 01531 650020

## WOOD

Chatsworth Carpenters
Chatsworth Estate
Bakewell
Derbyshire
Tel: 01246 565300

Andrew Crace
Bourne Lane
Much Hadham
Hertfordshire SG10 6ER
Tel: 01279 842685
Fax: 01279 843646

Lister Lutyens Co. Ltd
Hammonds Drive
Eastbourne
East Sussex BN23 6PW
Tel: 01323 431177
Fax: 01323 639314
Email: sales@lister-lutyens.co.uk
www.lister-lutyens.co.uk

## COVERED SEATS

Stuart Garden Architecture
Burrow Hill Farm
Wiveliscombe
Somerset TA4 2RN
Tel: 01984 667458
Fax: 01984 667455
www.stuartgarden.com

## HAMMOCKS

Rusco
Little Faringdon Mill
Lechlade
Gloucestershire GL7 3QQ
Tel: 01367 252754
Fax: 01367 253406
Email: rusco@lfm.co.uk
www.lfm.co.uk

## DECKCHAIRS

Southsea Deckchairs
Portsmouth
Hampshire PO3 5LZ
Tel: 01705 652865

Southend Deckchair Co
Vanguards
Vanguards Way
Shoeburyness SS3 9QJ
Tel: 01702 294999

## PLASTIC

Garland Products Ltd
Ingswinford
Brierley Hill
West Midlands DY6 6TZ
Tel: 01384 278256

# THE WORKING GARDEN

*It is hard to know why so few modern gardeners grow their own vegetables. It is not a colossal amount of work and the rewards are immense. With decent garden features the working garden can look good too. Modest nineteenth-century suburban gardens usually kept flowers in the front 'show' gardens and grew fruit and vegetables in the back. So give yourself a vine pergola and imagine yourself in ancient Pompeii.*

## WATERING CANS

Hawes Watering Cans
Haws Elliott Ltd
Smethwick
West Midlands B67 5AB
Tel: 01214 202494

## WATTLE PANELS

English Hurdle
Curload
Stoke St Gregory
Taunton
Somerset TA3 6JD
Tel: 01823 698418
Fax: 01823 698859
Email: hurdle@enterprise.net
www.hurdle.co.uk

## SHEDS

Tunstall Garden Sheds
Tunstall
Stoke-on-Trent
Staffordshire ST6 6AD
Tel: 01782 832166

Sheds & Shelters
Upper Street
Hollingbourne
Maidstone
Kent ME17 1UT
Tel: 01622 880031

Skindles Sheds & Fencing
Bromeswell
Woodbridge
Suffolk IP12 2PT
Tel: 01394 460581

## ANTIQUE TOOLS

Jenny Walker's Potting Shed
5 Montpelier Mews
Harrogate
North Yorkshire HG1 2TQ
Tel: 01423 526988

The Garden Shop
Shalesmoor
Sheffield
South Yorkshire
Tel: 01142 493629

## BELL JARS AND LANTERN CLOCHES

Garden Images Ltd
Highfield House
Wawensmere Road
Solihull
West Midlands B95 6BN
Tel: 01564 794035
Fax: 01564 794756

Queenswood Garden Centre
Wellington
Herefordshire HR4 8BB
Tel: 01432 830015
Fax: 01432 830833
www.queenswood.co.uk

The Traditional Garden Supply Company
The Square
Stow on the Wold
Gloucestershire
Tel: 01451 830345
*Customer enquiries:*
Tel: 08705 449449
*Mail order:*
Tel: 08706 003366
Fax: 08705 44 98 00
Email: sales@scottsofstow.demon.co.uk

Martin Hibbitt
2 Union Place
Oswestry
Shropshire SY11 1HN
Tel: 01691 656152
Fax: 01691 680 340
Email:
MartinHibbitt@compuserve.com

## CERAMIC FORCERS

Richard Charters
Harehope Forge Pottery
Alnwick
Newcastle NE66 2DW
Tel: 01668 217347
Fax: 01665 510624
Email: charters@tagish.co.uk
www.tag.co.uk/harehope

## BEEHIVES

Parslow Apiaries Ltd
Bledlow
Princes Risborough
Buckinghamshire HP27 9PB
Tel: 01844 344948

Maisemore Apiaries
Maisemore
Gloucester
Gloucestershire GL2 8HT
Tel: 01452 700289

## BIRDHOUSES

Forsham Cottage Arks
Goreside Farm
Great Chart, Ashford
Kent TN26 1JU
Tel: 0800 163797
Fax: 01233 820157
Email:
cindy@forshamcottagearks.co.uk
www.forshamcottagearks.co.uk

## CANE IMPORTERS

Cane & Co
155 London Road
Hemel Hempstead
Hertfordshire HP1 2RE
Tel: 01442 252364

Johnson J & Sons
Station Road
Bangor on Dee
Wrexham LL13 0AB
Tel: 01978 361178

# GENERAL

## GENERAL ANTIQUES

Godwin & Godwin – garden and conservatory antiques
www.godwin-godwin.co.uk/

Lassco
Saint Michael's
Mark St.
London EC2A 4ER
Tel: 020 7749 9944
Fax: 020 7749 9941
Email: replicas@lassco.co.uk
www.lassco.co.uk

Architectural Heritage
Taddington Manor
Taddington, Nr Cutsdean
Cheltenham
Gloucestershire GL54 5RY
Tel: 01386 584414
Fax: 01386 584236
Email:
puddy@architectural-heritage.co.uk
www.architectural-heritage.co.uk

# INDEX

First published in 2000 by
Conran Octopus Limited
a part of Octopus Publishing Group
2–4 Heron Quays
London E14 4JP

www.conran-octopus.co.uk

Text copyright © David Stuart 2000

Design and layout © Conran Octopus 2000

*Project Editor:* Sue Seddon

*Senior Editor:* Muna Reyal

*Art Editor:* Mary Staples

*Picture Research:* Mel Watson

*Production:* Alex Wiltshire

British Library Cataloguing-in-Publication Data. A catalogue record for this book is available from the British Library

ISBN 1 84091 140 9

Colour origination by Sang Choy International, Singapore

Printed in China.

PICTURE CREDITS

The Publisher would like to thank the following photographers and organisations for permission to reproduce their work.

1 Jason Smalley; 2 Fritz von der Schulenburg/The Interior Archive/Designer: Jed Johnson; 4 Jerry Harpur; 5 Marianne Majerus/Designer: Lionel Stirgess; 6 Hugh Palmer; 7 left John Glover/Chatsworth, Derbyshire; 7 right Nick Meers/National Trust Photo Library/Moseley Old Hall, Staffordshire; 8 left Juliette Wade/Mr and Mrs Benyon, Bleak House, Staffordshire; 8 right Steven Wooster/The Garden Picture Library/Designer: John Brookes, Denmans; 9 Marianne Majerus; 10–11 Gary Rogers; 13 Modeste Herwig/Fenton House, London; 14 left Marianne Majerus/Coton Manor Gardens, Northampton; 14–15 Marijke Heuff/Park Rosendael, Holland; 16 Marianne Majerus/Museo Sorolla, Madrid, Spain; 16-17 Clive Nichols/Arrow Cottage, Herefordshire; 18 Gary Rogers/Pedrodvorets, Russia; 19 John Bethell/The Garden Picture Library/Villa Lante, Lazio, Italy; 20 Leigh Clapp/Designer: Ann-Marie and Dror Barkai, Queensland, Australia; 20-21 Derek Harris/National Trust Photo Library/Tatton Park, Cheshire; 22 Ron Sutherland/The Garden Picture Library/Designer: A. Paul; 23 Deidi von Schaewen; 24 left Jill Ranford/Ffotograff; 24 right Jerry Harpur/Coldspring, New York, USA; 25 Jim Holmes/Axiom Photographic Agency; 26 left Clay Perry/The Garden Picture Library/Buscot Park, Oxfordshire; 26 right Marijke Heuff/Buscot Park, Oxfordshire; 27 above Hugh Palmer/Buscot Park, Oxfordshire; 27 below Marijke Heuff/Buscot Park, Oxfordshire; 28–29 John Glover/The Garden Picture Library; 31 Modeste Herwig; 32 left Marianne Majerus/Designer: William Woodhouse; 32–33 John Ferro Sims/The Garden Picture Library/Villa Carlotta, Italy; 33 John Glover/The Garden Picture Library/Toad Hall, Berkshire; 34 John Glover/'Hakone', Saratoga, California, USA; 34-35 Deidi von Schaewen; 36 Michel Viard/The Garden Picture Library/Designer: Roberto Burle Marx; 36–37 Linda Burgess/The Garden Picture Library/Regents Park, London; 37 Juliette Wade; 38 Marijke Heuff/Huis Bingerden, Angerlo, Holland; 39 Gary Rogers; 40 left Beatrice Pichon-Clarisse/Jardin du Prieure N.D. d'Orsan, France; 40–41 Marianne Majerus/Designer: Julia Brett; 41 Hugh Palmer/Nemours, Delaware, USA; 42 Marijke Heuff/Het Loo, The Netherlands; 42–43 J C Mayer – G Le Scanff/Het Loo, The Netherlands; 43 Marijke Heuff/Het Loo, The Netherlands; 44 Gary Rogers; 47 Modeste Herwig/Polesden Lacey, Surrey; 48 J C Mayer - G Le Scanff/Designers: Eric Ossart, Arnaud Maurieres,Jardin des Fournials, France; 48–49 Mick Hales/Designer: Roberto Burle Marx; 49 Erika Craddock/The Garden Picture Library/Yuyan Garden, Shanghai, China; 50 left Marianne Majerus; 50 right Marianne Majerus/Elton Hall, Herefordshire; 51 Hugh Palmer/Deans Court, Wimborne Minster, Dorset; 52 above S & O Mathews; 52 below Marianne Majerus/Designer: George Carter; 53 John Glover/The Garden Picture Library; 54 John Glover/Filoli Garden, California; 55 Erika Craddock/The Garden Picture Library/Suzhou, China; 56 Gary Rogers; 57 Marianne Majerus/Designer: Mirabel Osler; 58 left Ron Evans/The Garden Picture Library/Abbotswood, Gloucestershire; 58 above right Marianne Majerus/Designers: Emma & Jeff Follas; 58 below right Beatrice Pichon-Clarisse; 59 Ian Smith/Acres Wild Garden Design; 60-61 Nick Meers/The Garden Picture Library/Misarden Park, Gloucestershire; 61 above right John Glover/Designer: Chris Jacobsen, San Francisco; 61 below Rex Butcher/The Garden Picture Library; 62 Andrew Lawson/Hestercombe, Somerset; 63 Hugh Palmer/Giardino Giusti, Italy; 64 above left Natalie Tepper/Arcaid/Designer: Frank Lloyd Wright; 64 below left Richard Bryant/Arcaid/Designer: Frank Lloyd Wright; 64–65 Richard Bryant/Arcaid/Designer: Frank Lloyd Wright; 65 below Richard Bryant/Arcaid/Designer: Frank Lloyd Wright; 66–67 Stephen Robson/National Trust Photo Library/Ham House, Surrey; 69 Roger Foley/Colonial Williamsburg, USA; 70 Derek St Romaine/Helmingham Hall, Suffolk; 71 Andrew Lawson/Designer: Rosemary Verey; 72 Gary Rogers/Designer: Marc de Winter, Belgium; 72–73 Hugh Palmer/Kirby Hall, Northants; 74 left Andrew Lawson; 74 right Steven Wooster; 75 Derek St Romaine; 76 Deidi von Schaewen/Jardin de la Gaude, France; 76–77 Stephen Robson/National Trust Photo Library/Glendurgan, Cornwall; 77 above Marianne Majerus/Garden Picture Library/Chenies Manor, Buckinghamshire; 78–79 Hugh Palmer/Haseley Court, Oxfordshire; 80 Henk Dijkman; 83 J Sira/The Garden Picture Library/Batsford Arboretum, Gloucestershire; 84 Mark Bolton/The Garden Picture Library; 84–85 Steven Wooster/The Garden Picture Library/Mien Ruys Garden, Holland; 85 Gary Rogers/Stone House Hotel, East Sussex; 86 Gary Rogers/Lomonosov, St. Petersburg, Russia; 87 above Marijke Heuff/Mr J. Nieuwenhuis, Holland; 87 below Hugh Palmer/Antony, Cornwall; 88 Hugh Palmer/ Hartwell House, Buckinghamshire; 89 Clive Nichols/Artist: Patricia Volk/Hannah Peschar Gallery, Surrey; 90 Gary Rogers; 91 above Gil Hanly/Artist: Jeff Thomson, New Zealand; 91 below John Glover/Artist: Rupert Till, Old Place Farm, Kent; 92–93 Andrew Lawson/ Designer: Penelope Hobhouse; 93 above Marijke Heuff/Huys de Dohm, Heerlen, Holland; 93 below S & O Mathews/Brook Cottage, Oxfordshire; 94 Andrew Lawson/Chelsea Flower Show 1995; 95 above left Gary Rogers; 95 above right Gary Rogers; 95 below S & O Mathews; 96 Roger Foley/Landscape Architect: Mark Lapierre, USA; 97 Vera Collingwood/National Trust Photo Library/Cliveden, Buckinghamshire; 98 Marianne Majerus/Port Lympne, Kent; 99 left Clive Nichols/Designer: Mike Cedar/Construction by: Rebecca Keast; 99 right Jim Holmes/Axiom Photographic Agency; 100 above Heather Angel/Villa Garzoni, Italy; 100 below Gary Rogers/Villa Garzoni, Italy; 100–101 centre Hugh Palmer/Villa Garzoni, Italy; 101 Michele Lamontagne/Villa Garzoni, Italy; 102–103 John Glover/Chanticleer, USA; 105 Marijke Heuff/The Garden Picture Library/Mrs Goossenaerts, Miedema, Holland; 106 Sunniva Harte; 107 left Marijke Heuff/Park Rosendael, Holland; 107 right Hugh Palmer/Villa Garzoni, Italy; 108 Heather Angel/Sushou, China; 109 Juliette Wade/Diana Yakeley, London (NGS); 110 above Georgia Glynn Smith/The Garden Picture Library; 110 below Modeste Herwig/Broughton Castle, Oxfordshire; 110–111 Marijke Heuff/Walda Pairon, Belgium; 112 Marianne Majerus/Rousham House, Oxfordshire; 112–113 Marijke Heuff/The Garden Picture Library; 113 John Glover/De Melietuin, Holland; 114 left Steven Wooster/The Garden Picture Library; 114 right Andrew Lawson; 114–115 Andrea Jones/Garden Exposures/Lost Gardens of Heligan, Cornwall; 116 above Modeste Herwig/Designers: Henk and Paul Weijers; 116 below Lynne Brotchie/The Garden Picture Library; 117 S & O Mathews/Little Court, Hampshire; 118–119 Christopher Gallagher/The Garden Picture Library/Quinta dos Azulejos, Lisbon; 120–121 Claire de Virieu/Chateau Brecy, Normany; 123 Juliette Wade/Sir Anthony and Lady Bamford, Daylesford House, Gloucestershire (NGS); 124 left Stephen Robson/National Trust Photo Library/Tatton Park, Cheshire; 124–125 Hugh Palmer/Herrenhausen, Germany; 125 Andrew Lawson; 126 Gary Rogers; 127 left Jacqui Hurst/Artist: Janet Allan; 127 right John Glover; 128 Andrew Lawson; 128-129 Jacqui Hurst/Gibberd Garden, Essex; 129 Clive Nichols/Hampton Court Flower Show 1998, Design: Natural and Oriental Water Gardens; 130 Jacqui Hurst; 130–131 S & O Mathews/Pashley Manor, Sussex; 131 Clive Nichols/Chelsea Flower Show 1999/Designer: Michael Balston, The Telegraph Reflective Garden ; 132 Clive Nichols/Chelsea Flower Show 1999/Designer: Sir Terence Conran, The Chef's Garden Roof Garden; 133 left Andrew Lawson/Lord Leycester Hospital, Warwick; 133 right Andrew Lawson; 134 left Andrew Butler/National Trust Photo Library/Powis Castle, Wales; 134 right Andrew Lawson/Powis Castle, Wales; 134-135 Andrew Lawson/Powis Castle, Wales; 135 Andrew Butler/National Trust Photo Library/Powis Castle, Wales; 136 Andrea Jones/Garden Exposures; 139 J C Mayer – G Le Scanff/Jardin des Paradis, (81) Cordes-sur-Ciel, France; 140 above Juliette Wade/Priory d'Orsan, France; 140 below Marianne Majerus; 140-141 Gary Rogers/Designer: Marc Schoellen; 142 Marianne Majerus; 143 left Juliette Wade/The Garden Picture Library; 143 right Sunniva Harte/Apple Tree Cottage, West Sussex; 144 J C Mayer – G Le Scanff/Domaine de St. Jean de Beauregard.(91) France; 145 left Stephen Robson/Gunilla Pickard, Essex; 145 right Jacqui Hurst/The Garden Picture Library; 146 left Deidi von Schaewen; 146 right John Glover; 147 Sunniva Harte/Firle Place, East Sussex; 148 Andrew Lawson/ Kellie Castle, Scotland; 148-149 John Glover/Designer: Alan Titchmarsh; 149 Jerry Harpur/Designers: Oehme and van Sweden, Washington DC, USA. Owner: Michael Robinson; 150–151 Mick Hales/Designer: Frank Cabot, Les Quatre Vents, Quebec, Canada.